P9-ELO-447

Back Row, left to right:
Dan Driessen, Darrel Chaney, Ken Griffey, Gary Nolan, Dave Concepcion, Ed Armbrister,
Clay Carroll, Will McEnaney, Terry Crowley, Cesar Geronimo, Don Gullett.

Middle Row:
Bernie Stowe, Equipment Manager; Paul Campbell, Traveling Secretary; Johnny Bench,
Bill Plummer, Clay Kirby, George Foster, Jack Billingham, Tom Carroll, Pat Darcy, Rawly Eastwick,
Tony Perez, Pedro Borbon, Larry Starr, Trainer.

Front Row:
Pete Rose, Joe Morgan, Ted Kluszewski, Coach; Alex Grammas, Coach; Sparky Anderson,
Manager; George Scherger, Coach; Larry Shepard, Coach; Fred Norman, Doug Flynn,
Merv Rettenmund. Seated in front: Tim McGinn, Bat Boy.

Dad,
Happy Fathers Day
1979

Wanted to get this book a
long time ago for you
but the Reds were doing
so great they wanted to
much money for it.
Found it on sale — so
enjoy reading it.
a little outdated but good anyway

Love,
Nancy
Barry
&
Heidi

THE
BIG RED
MACHINE

THE BIG MACH

PRENTICE-HALL, INC

RED
LINE

Bob Hertzel

Englewood Cliffs, New Jersey

THE BIG RED MACHINE, by Bob Hertzel

Printed in the United States of America
Prentice-Hall International, Inc., London
Prentice-Hall of Australia, Pty. Ltd., Sydney
Prentice-Hall of Canada, Ltd., Toronto
Prentice-Hall of India Private Ltd., New Dehli
Prentice-Hall of Japan, Inc., Tokyo

10   9   8   7   6   5   4   3   2

Library of Congress Cataloging in Publication Data
Hertzel, Bob.
The Big Red Machine.
1. Cincinnati. Baseball club (National League)
I. Title.
GV875.C65H47   796.357'64'0977178   75-45010
ISBN 0-13-076190-7

DEDICATION

TO ROBBY, AMY, and CHRISTOPHER,
small people who stand as tall as The Big
Red Machine in my eyes.

Contents

Introduction

The history of baseball is brightened by an abundance of colorful nicknames. A player does not enter the game without someone, somewhere, hanging upon him a name that, like it or not, stays with him until it is last written in his obituary.

George Herman Ruth was Babe. Lou Gehrig was The Iron Horse. Ty Cobb was The Georgia Peach. Tris Speaker became The Gray Eagle and Joe DiMaggio was Joltin' Joe or The Yankee Clipper.

The nicknames came perhaps from something physical. Mordecai Brown was Three-Finger Brown because of a physical disability. How many men named Lefty played the game? How many guys called Red were there?

Anything could lead to the birth of a nickname. Ewell Blackwell was tall and slender and threw with a terrific sidearm motion. He became The Whip. Could you call Ted Kluszewski, with those massive arms bulging out from under cut off sleeves, anything but Big Klu?

Nicknames are not the sole property of baseball's

legendary past, days when sportswriters spent hours sitting in press boxes dreaming up colorful monickers. They are as much a part of today's game as AstroTurf, the slider, and the designated hitter.

At St. Louis, there is a relief pitcher named Al Hraboski. He is The Mad Hungarian. Pete Rose is and always will be Charlie Hustle. Carl Yastrzemski had to become Yaz. There is Catfish Hunter and Blue Moon Odom, and Nolan Ryan was dubbed Ryan's Express.

But baseball players are not the only ones who over the years have been singled out to be called by something other than their given names. Teams are also so honored and when a title is bestowed upon a team, it will live forever in the hearts and minds of those creatures who are the baseball fans.

The 1927 New York Yankees are generally considered the best team ever to play the game. They combined pitching and defense with an awesomeness not known in that day. They became Murderer's Row. The name itself seems to spit forth terror. Murderer's Row. Ruth. Gehrig. Tony Lazzeri. Bill Dickey. Bob Meusel. It stood for destruction and for domination of the sport.

The zany St. Louis Cardinals of the 1930s were The Gas House Gang. They were good, but they were also wacky, headed by the Number 1 oddball in the game, Jerome Hanna Dean, who could not miss being Dizzy. Frankie Frisch was the manager, himself the owner of the colorful nickname, The Fordham Flash, echoing his collegiate background in an age when baseball players seldom attended college, and from a speed of foot that put him out of the ordinary.

There was Pepper Martin and Joe Medwick, called Ducky. They laughed and joked and pranked their way into baseball lore, forever remembered.

2

The Brooklyn Dodgers of the 1940s and 1950s somehow escaped being tagged, despite their brilliance and despite nicknames that included Pee Wee and Preacher and Skoonj and Shotgun. For twenty years, they were nothing but the Brooklyn Dodgers. Then, in the 1970s, along came the most literate of sportswriters to write a best selling book. Roger Kahn made the Brooklyn Dodgers into The Boys of Summer, a name that surely will endure.

The 1970s so far have been dominated by a team from the West, the Oakland Athletics, winners of three consecutive world championships. It is a colorful team owned by a colorful man, Charles O. Finley, and filled with colorful players. But somehow they have remained nameless, the closest thing to a nickname being The Fighting A's, a reference to the players' propensity for fighting among themselves. The name, though, didn't catch on. The A's, dressed in the brightest of uniforms, wearing the most flamboyant of mustaches, pulling off the most irrational of stunts, have never captured the imagination of the sporting public. Their own fans stay away from the ball park as if there actually were something better to do in Oakland than go to the ball game. Success on the field did not breed a legend.

There is, however, a legendary team of the 1970s. It lives of all places in Cincinnati, Ohio, a conservative Middle Western community of German ancestry. It is an industrial community located on the Ohio River where Ohio, Indiana, and Kentucky seem to become one. It is, in the ever-expanding big league scene, the third smallest of major league cities. It is also the best baseball city anywhere.

In this setting in the year 1969 there was born the legend. The Cincinnati Reds died a painless death and became to all, The Big Red Machine.

The Big Red Machine.

It has a menacing ring to it. It sounds as it should. It became the rallying cry for a legion of fans—not only in Cincinnati, but in a surrounding area of 150 miles. They love their Big Red Machine and, to be honest, the men who make up The Machine take a certain pride in the name itself, as those Yankees of the 1920s must have taken pride in being called Murderer's Row.

The name sounds as if it came straight out of J. Walter Thompson's advertising firm in New York, the creation of some advertising copy writer. But it came from no such source. The fact is that it is difficult if not impossible to pin down the creation of The Big Red Machine because two men claim credit for its creation. They are men who are as different as night and day. One man is a player on The Big Red Machine, a man who makes his living with his physical skills and not his mental agility. The other is a sportswriter who lives by the catchy phrase, the turn of a word.

Pete Rose, captain of The Big Red Machine, says he was the first man ever to call the Cincinnati Reds The Big Red Machine. Bob Hunter, baseball writer of the Los Angeles Herald-Examiner, *says it was he. "I originated the name," says Rose, openly defiant. "Hunter? No way. It was at Crosley Field and I started calling us the Big Red Machine. At the time, I had this red thirty-four Ford. That, I said, was the Little Red Machine and the team was the Big Red Machine." A comparison to his antique car, that is how Rose says he came up with the name.*

"I hear Rose is claiming it," says Hunter, "but I gave them the name." Bob Hunter remembers well what happened. "The Reds had just finished winning a game 19-17, from the Philadelphia Phillies. I thought about the color of the uniforms and the power they had. They were like a machine, big and red. That's how it came about."

Around that same time Bob Hunter was dreaming up

4

nicknames as if he were a Hollywood press agent. The best he hung on Bill Singer, then a 20-game winner with the Los Angeles Dodgers. Hunter took one look at Singer, a hard thrower, and began calling him The Singer Throwing Machine.

When the Reds arrived in L.A. after the 19-17 shootout in Philadelphia, a game which was won, coincidentally, when Rose made a diving catch in right field with the bases loaded for the final out, Hunter wrote of the invasion of The Big Red Machine.

Arriving at the park that afternoon, Dave Bristol, then manager of the Reds, came up to Hunter. "Big Red Machine," said Bristol. "I like that. I like that. Keep using it."

"That," said Hunter, "convinced me to keep on with it."

Hunter or Rose. Rose or Hunter. Does it matter? Whichever, it was picked up. Before long, everyone was talking of The Big Red Machine, sometimes shortening it to BRM for headlines. And the public knew what the BRM stood for.

New York— "Big Red Machine Faces Mets," read the headlines. Cincinnati— "The Big Red Machine Chugs On," said the headlines. Everywhere the same thing. The ball club knew a good thing when they saw it. They gobbled the name up, applied for a copyright on it, and were granted it. They used it in their promotions. The Big Red Machine became a salable commodity.

Jerry Dowling is the sports cartoonist for The Cincinnati Enquirer. It was he who drew the original caricature of The Big Red Machine. It appeared in 1969, as did the nickname. The first one was a tractor-like vehicle with Pete Rose, Johnny Bench, and Dave Bristol aboard. Rose and Bench were feeding baseballs into it for fuel and it was spouting out home runs.

5

"I must have made three thousand dollars off *The Big Red Machine* cartoon," says Dowling. "I've drawn about fifty different versions of it." Dowling's *Big Red Machine* cartoons have appeared on the cover of a record album, the cover of a coloring book, which, when the Reds blew the 1972 World Series, never was released, and on two collector's whisky bottles. The Reds are even considering putting out a limited edition print of Dowling's *Big Red Machine*.

The Big Red Machine caught on everywhere. But it did not win the pennant in 1969, its faulty pitching costing it down the stretch in the first divisional race in baseball history. In 1970, *The Big Red Machine* reached the pinnacle of its fame. Sparky Anderson was named manager and the team was ready to explode. And explode it did. It won seventy of its first one hundred games and had the Western Division all but clinched by the All-Star break.

Rose and Bench, Tony Perez and Lee May, Bobby Tolan. They became household words around America. But alas, the Machine ran out of gas. Its pitchers crippled, it lost the World Series to Baltimore and Brooks Robinson.

In 1971, *The Big Red Machine* was in dire need of an overhaul. The pitching staff became one unending sore arm, and Tolan ruptured his Achilles tendon, missing the entire season.

"They started calling us *The Little Red Wagon*," recalls Rose with a laugh.

Then came 1972 and the overhaul. Joe Morgan, Jack Billingham, Cesar Geronimo, and Denis Menke came in to add the new parts. The team went into overdrive and won the pennant, went to the seventh game of the World Series, then lost to the A's.

Favored in 1973, they won the West with a dramatic late run at the Los Angeles Dodgers, ignited when an obscure catcher named Hal King hit a three-run homer with two out in the bottom of the ninth inning, the Machine trailing Don Sutton 2-1. The Reds made up ten and a half games and captured the public's imagination as well as the division title.

But again the big one evaded them. The New York Mets, a team given no chance in the playoffs, pulled the upset of upsets in a series remembered most for the fight between Rose and Bud Harrelson at second base in game Number 3. As the 1974 season opened, The Big Red Machine got off to its usually slow start, fell ten and a half behind Los Angeles and then made its late rush. The Dodger lead decreased daily. "They may be in first place but they're chasing us," observed Rose.

L.A.'s lead dwindled to a game and a half and then the Dodgers, head-to-head, beat the Reds. The miracle couldn't be pulled off. Again, the team that was acknowledged as having the best talent in baseball, the team that was the legend, lost an important one. The reputation was there. The Big Red Machine did not win the big game. It bothered the players who have pride in their ability and pride in the nickname itself.

When 1975 came around, the Reds, highly-paid and successful, were still a hungry team. They had something to prove and prove it they did, annihilating the Dodgers. annihilating the world.

The Big Red Machine. It was at its awesome best, blending speed and power, pitching and defense, and that intangible, pride. Being a part of The Big Red Machine meant something to the men involved. "I took pride in the name before I even came to Cincinnati," says Little Joe Morgan, the do-everything second baseman who is credited with being the man who gave the Machine all that it was lacking. "But, to be honest with you, I didn't help build the name. That bothered me a little when I first got here. The first thing I did was go out and get me one of those Big Red Machine T-shirts. I'd wear it every day under my uniform. It helped make me feel like I belonged. Now I don't feel like I need it. I feel like I belong. It's sort of like being with the old Yankees; you took pride because there was something there before you and now you were part of it."

Pride in being part of The Big Red Machine. That is what it is all about. And this then, is the story of The Big Red Machine, the men who are part of it and the man, Bob Howsam, who created it.

AT LAST, HEAVEN

Sparky Anderson was worried. Really worried. It was the seventh game of the 1975 World Series and his heavily-favored Cincinnati Reds had done no better than win three of the previous six games. He was not worried that his team was inferior to the Boston Red Sox. What he did worry about was that Boston was "a team of destiny." All series long, thirteen days of it, the thought had kept eating away at his mind. "All I could see," said the manager of Cincinnati's Big Red Machine, "was Boston being a team of destiny, just

9

like the Mets of 1969 when they beat Baltimore in the World Series."

The night before had done nothing to relieve Anderson's fears. That had been the sixth game, a game the Reds were supposed to win, a game they had . . . and a game they lost. They had led 6-3, just four outs from a world championship when Rawly Eastwick, a confident rookie right-hander relief pitcher who all season had been *the* man in the tough situations, served up a home run ball to Bernie Carbo.

The fact that Carbo hit a three-run homer, erasing that 6-3 Cincinnati advantage when the World Series seemed to belong to the victory-starved Reds, was not what hurt Anderson. What hurt him more was that he had not, at that particular point in time, gone to left-handed pitcher Will McEnaney, the man he had called on throughout the incredible season to retire left-handed hitters.

"I knew," said Anderson, "that if I'd gone to McEnaney Boston would have pinch-hit with Juan Beniquez." Beniquez is a right-handed hitter and, with "The Green Monster," Boston's short wall, looming just 315 feet down the left field line, any right-handed hitter is a dangerous hitter.

"If I'd brought McEnaney in and they'd gone to Beniquez and if he hit one over that damn wall, I would have been sick. I wouldn't have been able to live with myself." So Sparky Anderson, who earned the nickname Captain Hook for his reliance on his bull pen, for the quickness with which he got pitchers out of a game, stuck with Eastwick.

The count went to two balls and two strikes.

"Right then I thought about putting McEnaney in. I knew with a 2-2 count they wouldn't go to Beniquez. But I didn't do it," said Anderson.

10

The result was the three-run homer by Carbo. Bernie Carbo was a man Sparky Anderson had made into a major leaguer through careful handling when Anderson was a minor league manager, and Carbo was one of his players with a rotten attitude. A man Sparky Anderson had used brilliantly in 1970 as he brought the National League championship to Cincinnati in his first season as manager of The Big Red Machine. Bernie Carbo, a man Sparky Anderson had given up on by 1972. As a Red Carbo had been platooned, had been told he couldn't hit left-handers. But now Anderson refused to go with his gut intuition to bring in the left-hander to face Carbo because he feared something so inanimate as a thirty-seven-foot high wall in left field.

Sparky Anderson paid the price. Carbo slashed one into the centerfield seats and that tied the game. It gave Carlton Fisk his shot at fame.

In the twelfth inning of a four hour and one minute game that was as dramatic as any ever played in the World Series, including the seventh game of the 1960 World Series that was won by Pittsburgh on Bill Mazeroski's ninth-inning homer, Carlton Fisk came to the plate and hit a curve ball from Pat Darcy.

The baseball hugged the foul line, Fisk standing at the plate waving frantically to the ball in an effort to produce some kind of magic that would keep it fair. And fair it was, the baseball slamming into the foul screen, inches into fair territory for a game-winning home run.

It came as no surprise. Sparky Anderson saw it as another bit of destiny. "I was not worried about the Boston Red Sox," said Anderson. "But I'd confided to my coaches, I'd told them that the only thing that could beat us was destiny. I went over the two teams time after time. We went over them in our scouting reports. We looked at it objectively. We matched up the eight players and we came out with us ahead 6-1-1.

"Johnny Bench over Carlton Fisk. Tony Perez over Cecil Cooper. Joe Morgan over Denny Doyle. Davey Concepcion over Rick Burleson. Pete Rose over Rico Petrocelli. Ken Griffey over Darrell Evans, even though Evans was the surprise of the series to us. Yet, here we were 3-3. It was hard to believe."

It was not at all as Anderson had seen it and definitely not at all as any of the Reds had seen it. That the World Series, which started in Boston, had returned there was a surprise.

The Big Red Machine, a 3-to-2 favorite as the series opened, expected to win in five games. It did not in any way expect to return to Boston for a sixth game, much less a seventh. They had been propagandized—whether right or wrong matters not—that the National League is superior to the American League and they were the kings of the National League.

They had won their division by twenty games. No team since the 1906 Chicago Cubs, winners of an all-time record 116 games, had won a pennant race by twenty games. They had clinched the championship on September 7, earlier than any National League team in history. The Big Red Machine had won 108 games, which was more than any team since the 1909 Pittsburgh Pirates won 110 and which was the third highest win total ever put together in the National League. Now here they were going against a young, inexperienced, underdog Boston team, and The Big Red Machine was fighting for its life in a World Series that should have ended with nothing more than a Boston whimper.

The Reds were the team that had the reputation of *not* being able to win the big game. It was a reputation that

12

rankled, even though history said it was so. The last world championship Cincinnati had won was in 1940, a full thirty-five years earlier. In 1961 they had won a pennant but not a World Series. In 1970 and 1972 they won pennants and lost the World Series. In 1973 they won their division, yet the New York Mets, a team that was just four games over .500, won the playoffs. In 1974 they fell far behind the Los Angeles Dodgers, almost caught up, then faltered.

Now here they were again, with the seventh game of a World Series coming up. Overwhelming favorites were the Reds and Sparky Anderson was worrying about destiny. It was almost absurd. This superteam, better man for man, at least in their manager's eyes, were fighting for their lives, fighting Boston, fighting the fear of losing the big one again, fighting, perhaps, destiny.

The day of the seventh game of the World Series, Wednesday, October 22, dawned beautifully. It had been to the day, eight long months since the Cincinnati Reds had reported to spring training, just about 200 games had gone by, and now it was down to one game. The rains that had postponed game Number 6 for three boring days had gone and the sun shone brightly. For Sparky Anderson, though, it was a day in purgatory. The night before, after Carlton Fisk had hit the home run to make game Number 7 necessary, had been a rough one on the forty-one-year-old Cincinnati manager. He had not been able to fall asleep until four o'clock in the morning, thoughts of the previous six games and dreams of the seventh invading his tired mind. And when he awoke he could not understand it at all. He was soaked with perspiration. His sheets were soaked. His pillow was soaked. He had spent the night in a nervous sweat. "I didn't remember any dream," he was to recall, "but I must have had a nightmare."

Sparky Anderson's ulcers were acting up. At forty-one, he looked seventy, his face a road map of wrinkles, his hair pure white. Ray Shore, the Reds' super scout and the co-author of the scouting report on Boston with Rex Bowen, joined Anderson early in the morning. It had already been a brutal morning for Anderson. He left an eleven o'clock wake up call with instructions that he wasn't to be bothered with any other phone calls until then. At nine o'clock, his phone rang. Someone had gotten through, awakening him in his perspiration-soaked bed. A brunch was being given by the Red Sox for the press that afternoon. Shore told Anderson that he should attend. Anderson did not want to go. Shore persisted and Anderson gave in.

Sparky Anderson went. And he talked . . . and talked . . . and talked, as only he can. For two straight hours he sat there entertaining the press, admitting to previous mistakes, explaining his managerial strategy throughout the World Series, strategy that had been questioned by many. "That really helped, I have to admit it. I got rid of all my nervousness sitting there talking," said Sparky Anderson.

As Anderson spoke with the press in the Statler-Hilton, his players, too, were going through the final day of the season. At Howard Johnson's, down the street in room 1405, there was a poker game. Yes, even with the seventh game of the World Series coming up, the players were at ease enough to sit around and play poker.

Pete Rose and Johnny Bench. Terry Crowley, a reserve first baseman but mostly a pinch-hitter. Fred Norman, one of the starting pitchers. And Clay Kirby the forgotten man, a pitcher who had done little pitching all season.

They sat there and played poker and talked.

"Sparky ought to pitch me today," smiled Kirby, the only Cincinnati pitcher not to get into the World Series.

"Why?" asked Fred Norman.

"Because there's no way the Red Sox could have a scouting report on me. They haven't seen me pitch," answered Kirby with a laugh.

Johnny Bench was losing in the poker game. It didn't seem to matter, though, with the seventh game drawing nearer and nearer. He was asked about the Reds always losing the big one. Could this team, the superteam, recover should it lose this one?

"I don't know. I really don't know," said Johnny Bench, the superstar catcher. "I don't want to think about it. I don't want to think about losing."

Johnny Bench lost a little more money and suddenly it was time, time to go to the ball park, time to play the seventh game of the World Series, the game in which The Big Red Machine would either rule baseball or be laughed out of it.

There was nothing particularly different about the Cincinnati Reds' locker room before the game. There was the usual needling, Tony Perez and Joe Morgan going at each other, Pete Rose acting as the instigator.

Don Gullett seemed a bit uptight at being chosen to pitch the seventh game in a swirl of controversy. Gullett had had enough rest to pitch the sixth game, but Anderson bypassed him as he bypassed Jack Billingham, the second game winner.

Gary Nolan was Anderson's choice to pitch game Number 6, but he gave up a first-inning home run to Fred Lynn, setting the stage for the most exciting game of the World Series.

Don Gullett, 15-4 during the regular season and considered the best young pitcher in the game—Anderson had already predicted Gullett would make the Hall of Fame, even though the left-hander from Lynn, Kentucky, was

15

only twenty-four—was ready to pitch the seventh game.

Forty thousand fans at the minimum jammed ancient Fenway Park even though the announced attendance was 35,205. They came to root for their beloved Red Sox, to see if they were, indeed, the team of destiny. For a while it looked as if the Red Sox were.

Gullett, too rested, too strong, was having little trouble with Boston but he could not control himself. After two scoreless innings, Boston broke it open. Carl Yastrzemski, the most popular thing to hit Boston since the bean, drove in one run with a single and then Gullett, totally erratic with his fast ball, walked Rico Petrocelli and Dwight Evans with the bases loaded to force in two more runs. "I wasn't going to let up and let them hit it," Gullett was later to explain.

Now things looked bleak. Boston was ahead 3-0. Bill Lee, who they call "Spaceman" because he is a way out sort of character, was on the mound for Boston and the Reds were not exactly overwhelming him.

As they went into the fifth inning it was still 3-0. Then it happened. Davey Concepcion got an infield hit when Lee was late covering first base on a ground ball to Yaz. Ken Griffey then rifled one at second baseman Denny Doyle's feet. The ball was never touched by Doyle, going through for an error. Concepcion streaked into third base.

The Reds were alive, first and third, no one out. Calling upon every bit of resourcefulness he had, Lee got Cesar Geronimo to look at a third strike. In the dugout Sparky Anderson sent Merv Rettenmund up to pinch-hit for Gullett.

A fly ball would have meant a run. A base hit probably would have meant a rally.

But Merv Rettenmund hit into a double play. First and third, none out, and the Reds didn't score.

16

However, this was the turning point in the World Series, at least as far as Pete Rose, the most valuable player in the series, was concerned. "When Rettenmund hit into the double play," Rose explained, "he returned to the dugout. Most guys would go sit in the corner with their head hung low. Not Merv. He got in the dugout and started cheerleading as loud as he could. He carried it on all ballgame. It really helped us, really picked us up. If he wanted to win that bad, that his personal failure didn't matter, then we wanted to win that bad."

The next inning, the sixth, it finally happened. Rose led off with a single. Bench hit what seemed to be a routine double play ball to shortstop Rick Burleson, who fielded it cleanly and flipped it to the ill-fated Denny Doyle. Doyle seemed to hear Rose approaching, 200 pounds of muscle bearing down on him. Perhaps there were pictures flashing through Doyle's mind of Pete Rose smashing into Ray Fosse to win the 1970 All-Star game, or of Rose sliding hard into Bud Harrelson in the 1973 playoffs. Doyle leaped in the air to throw to first. Instead, he threw the ball into the Boston dugout.

"He just jumped," said Rose. "You can't jump and throw. You can't get the ball to the first baseman."

Instead of the inning being over the Reds had a man at second and two out, and Tony Perez at the plate. Tony Perez, trade bait over the winter as the Reds sought a third baseman to solidify their club. Tony Perez, off to a terrible start during the regular season, only to come on and drive in 109 runs, his ninth straight year of ninety or more RBIs, making him the only active player to accomplish that feat. Tony Perez, 0-for-14 in the World Series before hitting two home runs in the fifth game. Now he stood in against Lee.

Earlier in the game, Lee had thrown him one of his

blooper pitches—a slow, slow curve ball. Perez had taken it for a strike. Now as he stood ready he noticed something in Lee's windup, a little hesitation perhaps. It told Tony Perez the same slow curve was coming. Lee threw and Perez took the mightiest of swings. The ball left Fenway Park almost before Perez could leave the batter's box. It disappeared over The Green Monster, over the screen and into the darkness, landing somewhere on Ipswich Street. The 3-0 ball game was now 3-2.

The seventh inning came along. With one out Lee made the mistake of walking Ken Griffey, the speedy outfielder who had done so much for the Reds all season and who was to wind up scoring the Reds' final two runs of 1975. Bothered by a blister on the thumb of his pitching hand, Lee exited and left-hander Roger Moret was brought into the game.

While Geronimo was popping up, Griffey stole second base. It was the ninth straight base the Reds had stolen off Carlton Fisk who went into the series being compared to Johnny Bench as a catcher. "You don't want to embarrass anybody by comparing them to Johnny Bench," Sparky Anderson had said during the series.

Carlton Fisk now was embarrassed.

"We felt all along we could run on Boston. Other than Luis Tiant, they had no pitcher who could hold us close. Fisk is a fine catcher, but I don't think he's a power throwing catcher. And against an arm like his we can steal," said Anderson.

Griffey was at second, two were out and Ed Armbrister was sent up to hit for Jack Billingham, who had been brought in to relieve and done a superb job for two innings. Armbrister had been a center of controversy in the third game when he became entangled with Fisk on a bunt play;

18

Boston claimed interference but wound up only with defeat.

Armbrister, who had done whatever was asked of him all series long, drew a walk. First and second now, two out and Pete Rose the hitter. The situation was made for the man they call Charlie Hustle. He swung and sent a line drive screaming into centerfield. It fell in front of Fred Lynn as Griffey came home to tie the game.

"I was scared to death Lynn would catch that ball," said Rose. "They'd caught line drive after line drive on me all series. I think I would have flipped if Lynn had caught that one."

The game remained tied through the seventh, through the eighth, and now it was the ninth. Jim Burton, five days short of his twenty-sixth birthday, a left-hander, a rookie in a situation that was not built for a rookie, walked Griffey. Geronimo bunted him to second and Danny Driessen, hitting for Clay Carroll who was to be the winning pitcher, got Griffey to third with an infield grounder. Burton remained in the game as Pete Rose came to the plate. With first base open and the left-handed Joe Morgan due next it was thought Darrell Johnson would order an intentional walk to Rose. He went to the mound to talk to Burton. The decision was to pitch to Rose. The count went to 3-and-2. Burton threw a pitch that was high and outside, Rose starting to swing and then holding off. He had walked.

Now Joe Morgan was the hitter. Here was the man who had done it all for the Reds all season, the man who put the go in The Big Red Machine. And he had still one more thing to do.

He did it. He hit a looping fly ball to centerfield. Lynn could not get to it. It was a hit, Griffey trotting home with the run, the winning run. Two days earlier Fred Lynn would have caught Morgan's looper, having been playing

19

that shallow. But in the sixth game Fred Lynn crashed into the centerfield wall and the memory remained of the pain he had suffered. "He moved back after that," said Anderson. "He was a little shy of the fence. He didn't want to run into it again."

The Reds now had three outs to go to the championship. They remembered the sixth game and the late collapse. This time Will McEnaney was brought in to pitch and Beniquez was sent up to hit.

He didn't put the ball over The Green Monster. One out. Bob Montgomery then pinch-hit and grounded out. One out to go. Carl Yastrzemski stood between the Reds and heaven.

He swung hard, lofting a lazy fly ball to centerfield where Cesar Geronimo stood, the best outfielder in the game. "The only way he could have missed that ball would have been if he lost it in the sun and the sun went down seven hours ago," laughed Pete Rose. The ball settled into Geronimo's glove. Bench and McEnaney leaped upon each other. Rose joined in. Then Perez, then Morgan. They were going crazy in the middle of the field, crazy with joy.

A fan grabbed Bench's helmet; Bench put one of his giant hands around the fan's arm and quickly retrieved it. A fan tried to grab Bill Lee's cap. Losers don't grab. Lee hauled off and decked the fan.

Into the clubhouse went the joyous Reds, destiny on their side, at last the winner of the big game, world champions. Champagne corks popped. Players doused each other with the bubbly. And as they celebrated, the celebration began in Cincinnati. From all over they rushed to Fountain Square, horns blowing. One policeman was overcome by three men who took his gun. A woman's hair caught fire. The Cincinnati Reds' fans, so used to losing, now were letting off steam.

In the clubhouse it went on and on. Pete Rose had won the car as series Most Valuable Player and said, "I should chop it up and give a piece to everyone on the team. I couldn't be happier if I had all the money in the world." He went on and on. "Most clubs would have quit. Not this club. Not all year. We never quit. There were twenty-five heroes here." And the words continued to pour from Rose, a native of Cincinnati and veteran of thirteen years but never a champion. "Joe Morgan is my favorite player. He's great. Tony Perez is my favorite person. He's beautiful. Harmony, that's what won it for us."

"The frustration is over," said Morgan, standing in another part of the room. "At Houston I knew last place. When I came to Cincinnati I was disappointed when we didn't win. But now this. It was worth waiting for."

Will McEnaney and Rawly Eastwick, "The Kiddie Korps" relievers, hugged each other. "We're brothers," they said. "I can't believe it. What a year. What a rookie year," said Eastwick.

Johnny Bench took a swig of champagne. "This is the sweetest thing on earth," he said. "No matter what happens after this, I don't know if anything can top winning the series. Even if we win it again, they say the first time is always the sweetest."

"Now," added Morgan, "we can say we're the best. Before, we felt we were the best but couldn't say it because we hadn't won. Now, The Big Red Machine is the champion of the world."

And they dressed and flew home, a riotous flight with champagne and Bowie Kuhn, the commissioner of baseball.

Cincinnati. It welcomed The Big Red Machine unlike any other Cincinnati team had ever been welcomed. A parade. Fountain Square jammed with 15,000 people. And Pete Rose stood before the 15,000 and told them, "The championship is home where it belongs."

2

FROM SPARKY WHO? TO "CAPTAIN HOOK"

This was to have been a big day in the life of Sparky Anderson. It was October 8, 1969 and he was going to drive from his home in Thousand Oaks, California to Anaheim Stadium to formally sign his contract as third base coach of the California Angels.

A successful minor league manager, Anderson had spent the previous season coaching third base for the San Diego Padres. Now he was going to join Lefty Phillips, the man who signed him to his first contract and his mentor and guiding light throughout his non-distinguished playing career. Phillips was the manager of the Angels and Sparky Anderson figured the biggest break he'd ever gotten in his life was to be offered a job working under the man he idolized.

Anderson left his Thousand Oaks home at about eleven a.m. He drove to Eagle Rock which was home to Phillips and picked up his new boss. They were to meet Dick Walsh, the general manager of the Angels, in Anaheim to have lunch. The ride was uneventful, the talk naturally of baseball.

"You know," mumbled Lefty, who always mumbled, "the Reds fired Dave Bristol yesterday."

This news was of interest to Anderson. He had worked under Bob Howsam, the Cincinnati general manager, for four years, first as a minor league manager in the St. Louis Cardinal organization and then for a year in the Cincinnati organization.

"Who'd they hire?" asked Anderson.

"Nobody yet," said Phillips. "They said they have four or five people under consideration and that they wouldn't name a manager for a few days."

Sparky Anderson didn't give a whole lot more thought to the situation in Cincinnati. Heck, the last time he'd talked to anyone connected with the Reds was over a month earlier when San Diego made its last trip to town. Then he'd gone up and had a few words with Sheldon "Chief" Bender, the Reds' director of player personnel and not to be confused with the Hall of Fame pitcher, although he always is. The talk had been general.

Anderson and Phillips arrived at Anaheim Stadium and went to see Walsh. While waiting for the general manager to clear up the work in front of him Anderson

24

became involved in a conversation with Tommy Summers, the Angels' farm director. Already he was lending his knowledge to his new organization, telling Summers how spring training was run by the Cardinals and how the Cardinals—long known as leaders in the field of organization—had run their minor league system.

Anderson, Phillips, and Walsh then left for a quiet lunch. "While I've got you here," said Walsh over a cup of coffee, "you might as well sign this." He pulled from his breast pocket the contract for Sparky Anderson to sign, making him third base coach of the Angels. Anderson took pen in hand and in his barely legible scrawl wrote "George Anderson." It was now official.

Back to Angel Stadium the threesome drove, the conversation now turning to Alex Johnson. The Angels were in need of a hitter and Alex Johnson at Cincinnati was available. As they sat in Walsh's office around 2:30 p.m. discussing Alex Johnson, Walsh's phone rang. He began conversing with some party unknown to Anderson while Sparky continued telling Lefty what he thought the Angels would have to give up to pry Johnson, a noted .300 hitter and troublemaker, away from Cincinnati.

Finally, Walsh finished his conversation. He hung up the phone and looked at Anderson. "Sparky," he said, "how would you like to be manager of the Reds?"

Anderson felt his heart skip a beat. "Dick, don't kid me about something as serious as that."

"I'm not kidding," said Walsh. "That was Bob Howsam and he wants you to call him when you get home." Walsh noticed that the calm Anderson had displayed all day was rapidly evaporating into excitement. "Let's have some coffee, first. I don't want you to kill my manager on the freeway."

The ride to Lefty's house was a quiet one which was strange for Anderson, who has been known to carry on conversations with a telephone pole. Upon arriving in Eagle Rock, Lefty could take it no more. "Call from here," he commanded. "I can't wait an hour for you to drive home."

So Sparky Anderson, whose playing career in the big leagues consisted of one season as second baseman for the last-place Philadelphia Phillies, called Bob Howsam. He talked for what seemed to be forever, finally hanging up the phone. "They want me to be on a plane at one o'clock this morning," Sparky Anderson told Lefty Phillips.

"Congratulations," said Phillips. His pupil had finally arrived.

In Cincinnati there was some concern at the time. The decision to fire Bristol had been a difficult one. Plagued with a pitching staff that was crippled all season, the newly-named Big Red Machine had remained in contention until the final week. But it hadn't won and Bob Howsam was hungry for victory, especially with his team heading into its new stadium the following season, and with the coming year's All-Star game scheduled in the round jewel on the Ohio River.

So the decision was reached. Dave Bristol must go.

"I did not," says Howsam today, "have Sparky Anderson in mind at the time."

The Reds knew Bristol was a popular manager with the fans and even more so with his players, most of whom he had managed throughout their minor league careers. Howsam and his staff began discussing names. Four or five names were brought up. The best of the lot the consensus said, was George Lee "Sparky" Anderson.

There were still doubts even when the decision was reached. "Any time a person hasn't been in the major leagues," explains Howsam, "and is unknown, there has to be doubts. But, the thing about naming a fellow like that is you have to believe he can do the job and do it well enough to convince the fans he's a good manager, and the players that he uses the proper strategy. There are no guarantees. But we had confidence Sparky Anderson could do the job."

So that night, flying under the name of George Anderson, Sparky Anderson arrived in Cincinnati. "I didn't have to sneak in under an assumed name," Sparky says. "No one knew me anyway."

The next morning at a hastily summoned press conference, Sparky Anderson was introduced to the public as baseball's youngest manager, being just thirty-six years old, and as the forty-fourth manager in the history of the Reds, baseball's first professional team.

"Sparky Who?" screamed the headlines the next day. After all, this wasn't quite like hiring one of those major league bounce-around managers. Sparky Anderson was a total unknown.

And what the Reds got was something totally out of the ordinary, a man who was inheriting a team about to blossom into something extraordinary and who would handle it in his own way. He was a combination of a lot of things—Casey Stengel, Chuck Dressen, Preston Gomez, Lefty Phillips, and most of all, himself.

Sparky Anderson's grammar can best be described as early third grade. He doesn't stop at double negatives, he'll throw in a triple negative. His conversation is pure Stengelese, talking for fifteen minutes without ever answering the question put to him.

Anderson never was much in school.

"My spelling was so bad I was embarrassed by it," he recalls. "I never took a note, still don't, cause I can't spell things right."

Sparky Anderson's education, instead, was in the field

of baseball. He played on an American Legion team that won the national championship, along with Billy Consolo, once a Boston Red infielder; Anderson was good enough to bring the scouts knocking on his door. These, though, were pre-expansion days. Even though he had talent there was no commotion over him. There were only sixteen teams then and plenty of players to go around.

An hour after graduating from high school, Sparky Anderson sat down with Lefty Phillips, then scouting for the Brooklyn Dodgers, and signed a contract. He was not, he points out, a "bonus baby."

"I got three thousand dollars and that included my salary," he says.

As a baseball player Sparky Anderson was a very good manager. Oh, he could play defense and he was smart, right out of the Eddie Stanky-Billy Martin school. But he had one drawback. He couldn't hit.

His minor league averages weren't exactly what you'd call rock bottom, but then again, the pitching wasn't what you'd call major league. After six years of bouncing around in the Dodger chain with no future, he was traded to Philadelphia for Rip Repulski, Gene Snyder, and Jim Golden.

In 1959 Sparky Anderson became the regular second baseman of the Philadelphia Phillies, a team so bad that its own manager, Eddie Sawyer, during a clubhouse meeting called it "the worst team in baseball history."

The 1959 Phils finished last and so did Sparky Anderson. He played 152 games—naturally batting eighth. His batting average was .218 and he had but 104 hits, only twelve of them for extra bases. None was a home run.

"Home run?" he now laughs. "I never even hit the wall."

The record books for many years listed the name of George L. Anderson as the worst hitter ever to play 150 or more games in a season. Then along came a couple of guys named Dal Maxvill and Hal Lanier and they broke Anderson's records, hitting for a lower average and getting less hits.

The next season when Sparky Anderson was banished to the minor leagues the realization struck him that he never again would make it to the big leagues. He knew that he had been given his one chance as a player and had blown it.

It was difficult—no, make that impossible—in those early years to picture Sparky Anderson as a manager. His temper was legendary. During his first season he was thrown out of fourteen games. "I used to think that the umpires were out to get me," he remembers. "They'd blow a call and I'd go berserk."

Year after year it was the same thing. When he wasn't being pinch-hit for in the late innings, he was being ejected by an umpire. He had no control over himself, making it totally impossble for him to have control over others. But he was learning. Lefty Phillips was imparting to him his vast knowledge and Sparky Anderson was absorbing it all.

"I know this game because I learned it from Lefty," he says. "Lefty taught me everything there was to know about playing. I say Lefty Phillips had the greatest baseball mind I've ever seen. But he couldn't put his knowledge across talking to people. That's why he didn't make it as a manager. But he knew the game. I guess everyone's got to have a teacher and Lefty was mine."

Lefty Phillips is dead now, but at least to Sparky Anderson he is not forgotten.

Anderson's education continued under Chuck Dressen.

"Dressen was the best I've ever seen with pitchers," Anderson says. "He never made no mistakes in getting the pitcher out of there. He really knew what he was doing and I'd watch him and ask him a lot of questions. He'd always give an answer, too. I think he liked me asking the questions.

"He'd tell me if a pitcher started out throwing the ball high it was no problem. But if he starts out with the ball low, then begins throwing high, go get him. He's had it.

"He also taught me that you can let a starting pitcher pitch out of two jams, but don't let him pitch out of the third jam. I've let pitchers pitch out of a third jam sometimes and gotten away with it. But most of the time when I try, it backfires and I get burned."

Sparky Anderson knew his future in baseball was as a manager. The previous season at Toronto he hit only .249. He was given the chance to manage Toronto in 1964 and did a creditable job. His team finished with an 80-72 record, but was in fifth place.

What Anderson didn't know was that his life was about to be drastically altered. After the 1964 season the Toronto franchise was sold to millionaire Jack Kent Cooke. Cooke wanted his own manager and Sparky Anderson was fired, replaced by Dick Williams who gained his own share of fame as a manager after a mediocre playing career.

Sparky Anderson, the man with the child's temper, was out of baseball for the first time since high school graduation. And baseball was the only thing he knew. Sparky Anderson was frightened. What could he do? About the only skill he possessed outside of baseball was house painting, his father's profession, and he wasn't quite ready for that.

This is where Milton Blish entered Sparky Anderson's life. It was Milton Blish who Sparky Anderson remembered when his 1975 team won the playoffs from Pittsburgh. That victory was dedicated to Milton Blish, as was the world's championship that was to come later.

In a moment of happiness, as champagne corks were being popped all around him, Sparky Anderson thought of his friend back home in Thousand Oaks, California, cancer eating away at his spinal column.

"For the first time in my lifetime I am at total peace with myself," he said. "Through this terrible thing that Milton Blish is going through, I have realized that peace comes in a different way than just what we call false things like championships," he said as the celebration swirled around him. There was a touch of moisture in his eyes.

Throughout the season, throughout the playoffs, throughout the series, Sparky Anderson was on the phone a lot, calling the hospital, cheering Milton Blish, the man who had hired him so many years before when he was out of baseball and his future was dark.

"You're making it so much easier with your calls," Milton Blish told Sparky Anderson.

"Forget it," answered Sparky Anderson. "Real friendship means you don't ever have to say thank you." To Sparky Anderson nothing is more important than friendship.

"Friendship," he says, "walks with you."

It isn't a matter of picking up the telephone and calling. With Lefty Phillips it never was that way. Anderson could go all year without ever calling Lefty Phillips. But he was a friend.

Anderson remembered what Milton Blish did for him,

how the bank account was at zero and how it wasn't the easiest thing in the world to sell Ramblers in 1964. "He gave me every house deal he had," recalled Anderson. "That was an extra seven hundred or eight hundred a month." A house deal in the auto business is when an owner or sales manager sells a car where there is no compensation for the salesman. Blish was giving Anderson commissions on his house deals. Now, in the moment of triumph Sparky Anderson remembered his friend.

Given an income through the job provided by Milton Blish, Anderson began writing letters to every baseball team he could think of in hopes they had some kind of opening somewhere, anything to get back into the game.

"That experience made me a person," he says. "Before that I was cocky. I felt I could go it alone. But I learned I needed other people. Before that I never cared about nobody. I never cared what anyone thought. I grew up in a hurry."

Forces were at work at this time, though, to bring Anderson back into baseball. Bob Howsam had been named general manager of the St. Louis Cardinals during the summer of 1964 and had scored a tremendous come-from-behind victory to win the pennant. Now he was looking to improve the St. Louis farm system. He had an opening for a manager. He called, of all people, Dick Walsh, who then was with the Dodgers, and asked him if he knew of anyone at the time. Walsh said no.

"By gosh," Howsam now remembers, "the next day Dick called me back and said, 'I have a fellow I think you could use by the name of Sparky Anderson. Do you know him?'"

Howsam knew of him at least, that in 1954 he was a fiery minor league infielder at Pueblo, New Mexico.

32

Howsam asked Walsh for his recommendations on Anderson and they were all high. Howsam called Chief Bender into his office, told him about Anderson and about the qualifications Walsh had listed. "Let's get him," said Howsam. He picked up the phone, dialed the number, and handed the phone to Bender.

"We hired him right there," says Howsam.

Anderson, frightened at the prospect of being away from baseball, wasn't going to quibble over position or salary. The relationship between Bob Howsam and Sparky Anderson had begun. It is a relationship that today bubbles over with loyalty.

The point was never better proven than two days after the 1973 World Series. Dick Williams had managed Oakland to the championship, then resigned. At the time, Charles O. Finley, the flamboyant Oakland owner, gave his blessings.

He had another manager in mind. He made one of his many long distance phone calls, this one to Thousand Oaks, California, to the residence of George Anderson.

"I'd like you to manage my ball team," said Finley, his deep, gruff voice making it sound more like an order than an offer.

Sparky Anderson cut him short right there, telling him no thank you. "If I'd let him go on and make an offer, tell me what he was willing to do for me, it would have been tempting and it would be me just trying to find out what I could get," explains Anderson.

"I'm not interested at this time," Anderson said to Finley. "You do flatter me, telling me I'm the first man you offered the job to. But I'll never leave Bob Howsam. He brought me to the big leagues. He gave me a helluva club. I owe everything to him. I'll never even consider another offer until he tells me I'm through."

Finley did not seem shocked at the rebuff. To the contrary, he answered, "I'm sure glad there's still someone with integrity left in this game." A few days later Finley filed suit to keep Williams as his manager, successfully preventing him from taking a job as manager of the New York Yankees.

Sparky Anderson was something of a legend as a minor league manager. His first year in the Cardinal organization he was at Rock Hill, North Carolina. In the first half of the season his team finished eighth. "It didn't take me long to figure out they had sent me all the players they were considering releasing," he says.

Through some miracle, during the second half of the split season, he took his ragamuffin team and won the title with them. For four straight years Sparky Anderson managed a championship team in the minor leagues. Then came the beckoning from San Diego where he took the job as third base coach. Never again was he to return to the minor leagues.

Sparky Anderson had doubts when he took over the Reds in 1970. He was coming to a team that was star-studded in a league he only knew from the third base coaching box. He was worried about the reception he would get, both from the fans and the players.

During the winter of 1970, just prior to spring training, he came to Cincinnati to accompany the team on the caravan, a goodwill tour of Reds' country where the pitch is to sell tickets for the coming season, and give the local press some celebrities to write about, pushing basketball off the front pages of the sports section at least for a day.

The first stop was in Lexington, Kentucky. Pete Rose approached his new manager. "Look," said Rose, "I'm the highest paid player on this team and if you need anything done, come to me and I'll see it gets done."

"That," admits Anderson, "put me at ease. I knew I would be accepted." And Anderson has held Rose to his word. He has gone to him for help and Rose has always obliged.

"When things go bad, Pete'll come to me and say, 'Hey, I think you oughta hold a meeting and, if you want, chew my butt out. If you get on me, the others will listen.' And I've done it a couple of times, used him as the goat. It works. I admit it, I use some gimmicks with the boys but they're honest gimmicks."

Honesty is a big word to Sparky Anderson. He talks about managing in terms you seldom hear from a manager. They like to let you believe that Einstein invented baseball strategy and Freud developed the handling of players. Only *they* can do it. It is a theory that the baseball owners for years accepted, rehiring fired managers until it became almost a closed fraternity. Then along came Sparky.

"There ain't no genius who ever managed in this game," he crows. "I ain't no genius. No one is."

And he goes on. "Why am I smarter today as manager of the Cincinnati Reds than I was when I was a player or a minor league manager? Why am I smarter than some of my players? Because I'm the manager? No sir. Just because you're a manager don't make you no smarter than the next guy."

Sparky Anderson admits that a manager can lose games for a team, many more than he'll ever win. He admits that one man may fit a certain club and be able to handle it after having failed with another club. But a genius? That he won't buy.

Anderson, however, has proven himself to be something of a genius. "He absolutely amazes me," says Ted Kluszewski, one of Anderson's coaches and a man who has been around baseball in the big leagues since 1948. "He's always three batters ahead of the game. He's always thinking ahead, maneuvering the other team into a corner."

August 1, 1975 showed Sparky Anderson at his finest. He was matching wits with Walter Alston, the most respected manager in the game with twenty-four years service to prove the point. It was the Reds against the Dodgers, a showdown if you will, Cincinnati leading the West by fourteen and a half games and the Dodgers needing to sweep the three-game series that was just starting to have any kind of prayer of catching The Big Red Machine.

Don Sutton of the Dodgers and Jack Billingham of the Reds were locked in a pitchers' duel for five innings. In the sixth the Reds, claiming all game that Sutton had been doctoring the baseball with a piece of sandpaper tucked neatly away in his glove, got their wish. Plate umpire Bob Engel inspected the glove. He took five minutes to search Sutton. He found nothing.

However, Sutton must have been unnerved. Moments later Johnny Bench hit a three-run homer to give the Reds a 3-0 lead. In the bottom of the seventh the Dodgers came back with two runs to cut it to 3-2. In the eighth inning Anderson hit for the tiring Billingham and replaced him with left-handed pitcher, Will McEnaney.

With one out in the Dodger eighth, Alston pinch-hit for the left-handed Bill Buckner with right-hander Lee Lacy. Lacy got a hit. Alston went to his bench again, calling on right-hander Tom Paciorek to pinch-hit for John Hale.

Anderson now called in right-hander Rawly Eastwick, the Dodgers having taken two of their left-handed hitters out of the game. What's more, as the inning progressed the Dodgers hit for Steve Yeager, their catcher.

Everything was working for Anderson even though

the Dodgers did manage to tie the game. The Reds had a right-hander pitching and the Dodgers had only one left-handed hitter in the game. The Dodgers had stripped their personnel so badly that they wound up with Lacy, a second baseman, in left field and Paul Ray Powell, an inexperienced catcher who had never before handled a knuckleball, behind the plate trying to catch the elusive knuckleball of Charlie Hough.

Anderson sat back contentedly, knowing it was only a matter of time until he won the game. Sure enough, Powell let a wild pitch get past him. Then he had a passed ball. Two runners were moved into scoring position because of the catching change that was made. Fate, however, wasn't smiling on Anderson. Each man tried to score from second base on a single to Lacy in left field. Each man was thrown out at the plate by Lacy whose arm had to be suspect since he was not an outfielder.

In the bottom of the tenth it happened. Ron Cey hit a two-run homer and Anderson's tactics had been for nothing.

"That," said Anderson, "was the best game I ever managed."

It also showed the genius in his statement that "there ain't no genius who ever managed in this game."

Managing is a sometime thing. The right move is the one that works, the wrong move is the one that doesn't. Most managers go by "the book," a mythical table of percentages that says a left-handed pitcher is more effective against a left-handed hitter. Sparky Anderson has his own book. It is based on knowledge and, more often than not, is based on an out-and-out hunch.

"I will always leave myself wide open," he says. "I do what I think my club is capable of doing. What it can't do I try to stay away from. Sometimes, trying to stay away from something, I go against the book. People have been used to the stereotyped guy who never wants to put himself in the hole. A lot of managers never want to go out in front of 40,000 people and be the goat. They don't do the radical things, then they can't be blamed. They can say they played it by the book. Well, I don't manage that way. You have to accept criticism and the criticism will be there when you go against the book and fail."

The book, for example, tells a manager not to break up a winning combination. If a lineup works, stay with it. Sparky Anderson does nothing of the kind. If he's won four in a row with a given lineup, he's just as likely to change it the next day. It's the way he is.

Nothing, however, can display the daring and the genius of Sparky Anderson any better than the streak he engineered as he acquired the nickname Captain Hook, a name he now seems to cherish. On June 11, 1975 with the Reds a game and a half in front of the Los Angeles Dodgers, Don Gullett went all the way to beat the St. Louis Cardinals. The next complete game turned in by a Cincinnati pitcher came when Pat Darcy went the route on July 30. A full six weeks had passed between complete games.

Now when a manager has to go to his bull pen, it normally signifies that he is having troubles. So what happened during this streak of forty-five consecutive incomplete games—a major league record? The Reds' game-and-a-half lead grew to thirteen and a half. They won thirty-two and lost thirteen. Sparky Anderson, Captain Hook, used his bull pen to perfection. Sure, the starters at times resented it. But they were getting wins and the team was running away with the championship and everything was rosy.

Of course, everyone was happy when the streak ended.

As Anderson was to say, "It was becoming a monster to me."

The fans, secure in their lead over the Dodgers, were booing Anderson every time he stuck his head out of the dugout. And when it ended with Darcy beating San Francisco 6-1, they were rooting through the final innings as if he had a no-hitter working, cheering every strike.

Captain Hook through the season used Clay Carroll, Pedro Borbon, Rawly Eastwick, and Will McEnaney without fear, tossing the book out the window, forgetting the feelings of his starting pitchers. The result was that he was out in the open, easy to fire at, but his club kept winning.

There is more to managing, though, than just doing the right thing at the right time. There is a matter of handling players. "What Sparky Anderson does best," says Joe Morgan, "is keep us aiming toward one thing, winning."

Anderson's background blends into his managing. He has assets and he has liabilities. He knows it and discusses them freely. "My biggest fault is I really like ballplayers," he says. "I played and I was not a good player. I understand when you're not a good player how hard it is to try and keep playing. Like my one year in the big leagues. I wasn't kidding myself. I knew I wasn't any good. I knew I was never going to be able to hit. I understand these kids. I have a feeling for them. They don't think so when I send them back to the minor leagues, but I do understand.

"Take David Concepcion. I care about him. I get angry with him because, now that people really care, he has a tendency to go a little big time. I don't like to see people go big time. That's the hardest thing I fight against as manager. It hurts me to see guys who dreamed of being here, who were poor kids, come to the big leagues and let it go to their head.

"I know I've been told over and over not to get

39

involved in that stuff but it bothers me. I know they came here with nothing and I worry that when they're through they'll leave with nothing. I care about my players. It's just like with Ross Grimsley. He doesn't think I like him but I do. I like him because he'd take the ball every time I offered it to him. But he doesn't think I liked him because I didn't appreciate his goofiness."

Managing, even a team like the Reds that has been so successful since Anderson came on the scene, isn't always easy. Anderson has had his crises, one of them revolving around Grimsley, a talented, young, left-handed pitcher, one of the rarest commodities in baseball, who could not operate within the framework of the Reds. Grimsley battled the establishment. Anderson's rule against long hair and mustaches bothered him. One spring, he had to make three separate trips to a barber in one day until he got a haircut that pleased the manager. The two men, Grimsley and Anderson, drifted further apart until finally it was unworkable and Grimsley was dealt to Baltimore for Merv Rettenmund, a deal that backfired when Grimsley won eighteen games. "They don't win over there at Cincinnati because they worry about all the little things instead of worrying about how a player feels. They don't try to keep the players happy," said Grimsley.

"I'll be honest, I don't have no idea about handling players," admits Anderson. "I am strictly myself. I wouldn't know how to do it any other way."

Like all managers Anderson has rules. He rarely has problems with them. The reason is he seldom enforces them. "To me, I ask, are you looking to catch a guy so you can nail him on your rule or are you trying to get the most out of the guy? A lot of times I see things I don't see. I mean what is the point? Are you going out trying to catch people breaking your rules? If you are that's the easiest thing in the world. You can catch people all the time. I'm out to get the most out of that guy though.

"Some guys have to be pushed, to be checked. Others can go their own way. I think you have to adjust to the player, he don't have to adjust to you. I really don't like rules. If I have rules I have to worry about catching guys and that's not the answer to anything. There are certain guys who can stay out all night and burn the candle at both ends, but that's the only way they can play.

"The young guys, though, I try to check. I do get upset with them. The first couple of years up here if they're not watching they're gonna sink. They're not strong enough yet or they don't know themselves well enough to know when they can and when they can't go out. So that's why I watch them a little closer."

Rules. Anderson has the normal stuff — curfew, and so on. But he also has the classic rules of the conservative that he is. Hair kept short. Coat and tie on the plane. No alcohol on the plane. This in a day of personal freedom. And he gets away with it mainly because Pete Rose, Johnny Bench, and Joe Morgan will follow the rules.

"If Bench came to the park with long hair and a mustache what could I do? he asks.

Handling players, this is what really separates one manager from another. Another crisis centered around outfielder Bernie Carbo, at one time Anderson's pet project.

"I was closer to Bernie Carbo than any player I've ever had," says Anderson. "He's the only person since I managed that I feel I personally saved to be a player. I'll always have that feeling. My whole family has that feeling. They all loved Bernie because he was a part of me and because I worried about him so much at home. But he doesn't know that. Today he thinks I gave up on him."

When Anderson came into the Cincinnati organization as a minor league manager he was asked to go to the winter instructional league to observe. The team he observed included Carbo. It was a talented team. It was also a losing team.

Bernie Carbo, in those days, was called "The Village Idiot" by his teammates. He liked the nickname. He was, in baseball parlance, a flake and he had a terrible attitude. Anderson requested that Carbo be assigned to him at Asheville. One day, with Asheville in last place, Anderson walked down the left-field line with Carbo. "Bernie," he said, "do you care if the team wins or loses?"

"No," answered Carbo. "I only care if I get my hits."

"You'll see that's wrong," said Anderson, ending the conversation.

A couple of months later after Asheville had begun to win, Carbo came to Anderson. "Sparky," he said, "I now know what you meant. Winning makes everything in this game." Carbo's attitude had changed. By 1970 he was in the big leagues, playing left field for Anderson. He played well but all the while Anderson was catering to his every whim. The following season, 1971, Carbo started going badly.

"I knew I couldn't help him no more," said Sparky. "I knew if he didn't make a change and go somewhere else Bernie Carbo was through." Anderson stopped catering to Carbo and Carbo resented it. A year later he went to St. Louis, then on to Boston.

"I understand," Anderson now says. "At first it was hard for me to understand why players would get on me after I'd done things for them. But I understand. They're scared of failing. They have to blame someone and it's the manager, no matter who he is."

Sparky Anderson's final crisis centered around Bobby Tolan. A star in 1970, Bobby Tolan ruptured his Achilles tendon in the winter of 1971. He injured it playing basketball. Anderson and Howsam had gone on record objecting to their players playing basketball, but thanks to Marvin Miller they could not ban such an off-season activity.

Tolan fought back from the injury. In 1972 he made a spectacular recovery. He was Comeback Player of the Year. Then came 1973. Tolan got off slowly, Anderson maintains because he stopped working on the leg during the off-season, content that he didn't need it after his comeback the previous year.

Tolan became disgruntled. He put himself apart from his teammates who tried to understand him but couldn't. Tolan refused to take batting practice. He sat in the back of the dugout, not congratulating players on home runs. He jumped the club. He wanted to wear a mustache. Anderson would not allow such "radicalism" on his club. Tolan was fined and suspended. In the end, Tolan was traded to San Diego. He filed a grievance against the club and won it, having his fine returned. He never got the apology he demanded.

"Bobby Tolan," says Anderson, "was the biggest mistake I ever made as a manager. I think I might have saved him if I had lowered the boom right away. But I let it ride and it got out of hand. If only I had acted right away I might have saved him." But Sparky Anderson handles his players well. He starts with the stars of which he is overly blessed. These are the men who he feels must win for him. "Over the season it is the stars who do it, not the manager and not the fringe players," he says. He thinks about them and their well-being.

"When I came to the Reds in 1970, Tommy Helms had been a star player for a number of years. I never pinch-hit for him that whole season. I didn't want to humiliate him. If I had hit for him—and there were many times I thought it was the right thing to do—I would be humiliating him and humiliating all the rest of the guys by doing it. We were in front by ten games. It would have been different if we'd been in a tight race. But you can't have a guy lose face to his teammates in that situation."

Sparky Anderson thinks of Pete Rose.

"I would never humiliate Pete Rose," he says. "He's busted his butt, not only for me but for everybody for thirteen years. He doesn't deserve me belittling him. Every once in a while you've got to give him a little praise, make him feel appreciated. He needs it.

"I'll tell ya. If every guy cared about themselves and was an individualist like Pete, they'd be great players. When you're an individualist and you do good, you're not only helping one man. You're helping everyone. A guy like Pete won't go out and look bad. If you play like that you'll play good all the time. The guy that don't care if he looks bad, well, that guy's gonna look bad so often that you won't have to worry about him. He's gone. Pete, if he looks bad he's gonna go out and work at it. He does not want to be embarrassed."

Sparky Anderson knew all this when he approached Pete Rose about moving to third base this year. The Reds were floundering. They had no third baseman and the hitting was down. Here was Rose, an all-star outfielder, a former Gold Glove winner, a man who once had been moved to third base and failed so miserably that he lasted just sixteen games at the position.

Anderson asked him to move there just as Don Heffner had in 1966. Then, Rose sulked. This time he moved gladly and became perhaps the best third baseman in the league. It opened a spot for George Foster to play regularly and he became one of the Reds' top power hitters. Anderson had handled Rose and Rose, with respect toward the manager, had worked as hard as any rookie to learn the new position.

"I've been accused of a lot of things with Johnny Bench," says Anderson. "I've been called his daddy. But I really like the guy. Before I came to Cincinnati he used to talk to me a lot. He does things for me and I honestly believe he wouldn't do them for another manager. He does them because he likes me. Many's the time I've asked him to talk to some of the guys because I know a problem's coming. 'You're crazy,' he'll say to me. I'll say, 'John, it's gonna come.' He says all right, talks to the guy and the trouble will be headed off before it gets started."

Sparky Anderson's greatest bit of managing, though, may have been accomplished with Joe Morgan.

Morgan had a reputation as a troublemaker. He had not gotten along with Harry Walker, his manager in Houston, and it was said he was acting as a bad influence on Jimmy Wynn. Sparky Anderson went to Bernie Stowe, the Reds' equipment manager, and told him to put Morgan's locker right next to Rose's.

"I just felt, truthfully, that if they became friends, there never would be a problem with Joe Morgan," he said. They became fast friends. "I told Joe," recalled Anderson, "the longer you're around Pete the more you'll learn about how important it is to do your best every game, all game."

Sparky Anderson never mentioned Walker's name around Morgan. "I never wanted to go into that," Anderson remembers. "He's never brought it up to me and I don't want to delve into it. I know most guys like to be left basically on their own."

That's what Anderson did with Morgan. He also asked him to help out. He had him talk to Tolan when that trouble was brewing. It didn't work. He has had him working with pitchers, improving their pick-off move, and he's had Morgan working with base runners, improving their ability.

"I wanted Joe to feel like he had great knowledge. And he does. He could be a great manager some day." He also under Anderson has become a great player, something he never was before.

Sparky Anderson has certain views about managing a big league baseball team. Others may disagree. He changes pitchers when others wouldn't. He looks upon the bunt as if it were the plague. "Like a fighter, you always go with your strength," he says. "There are men on first and second, nobody out and Bench or Perez coming up. I say he hits. He may hit into a double play but he hits. If Bench and Perez don't hit I'm gonna die anyway."

Losing, to Sparky Anderson, is like dying.

"The ones that don't die a little bit, to me, never can be great," he says. "And winning, to me, that's the way you gotta live." Losing is the way you die. As a manager, losing destroys you and Anderson realizes that his day will come.

"You come with a bag and put it down in the office. Someday it will be time to leave and you pick up your bag and go. But it won't matter if you do your job honestly and fairly."

Anderson has done his job honestly and fairly. He has died very little, considering that during regular season play covering six years his record reads 581-383. In those six years he has won four division championships, three pennants, and to crown off the achievement, the 1975 world's championship.

Still, he remembers where he came from; the minor league background, the time out of baseball, the good fortune he had to be the right man in the right place. And, if he tends to forget for a moment, something always comes back to remind him.

His latest reminder came during the streak of incomplete games. As he made one of his numerous trips to the mound to remove a pitcher, the crowd gave forth with a tremendous boo. After the game, as he was driving home with his wife, Carol, and his three children, he was informed that his daughter, Shirlee, had been one of those booing him.

"And why would you boo me?" he asked.

"So all those people booing wouldn't know you were my father," she answered.

Sparky Anderson laughs when he tells the story. His feet, though, through it all have remained on the ground.

3

THE CREATION

Where does one go to find the creation of The Big Red Machine? Did it begin that day in 1959 when the Reds, as a favor to an old friend, signed a scrawny kid from the Western Hills section of Cincinnati?

The kid didn't hit very well and his speed was just average and his arm below average. All he had was a big heart and a desire to succeed. So the Reds coughed up a few bucks ("I signed my bonus check at the drug store") and signed Peter Edward Rose to a contract.

Was that the start of what was to be The Big Red Machine?

Or did the beginning come on that historic June day in 1965 when major league baseball conducted its first free agent draft? On that morning, after having named Bernie Carbo as their first draft pick ever, the Reds announced the selection of Johnny Lee Bench of Binger, Oklahoma.

Was that the start of what was to be The Big Red Machine?

In reality the Creation cannot be pinned down to one point in time, one moment. Instead, the building of the team was more like Michelangelo painting the Sistine Chapel. It was a tedious, cleverly-planned effort, each part being added little by little until, when it was done, perfection had been reached.

Any analysis, though, of the Creation always comes back to one man, to the Michelangelo of the Reds, to Robert Lee Howsam. It was his master plan that was carried out, his carefully laid groundwork that produced the grandeur of a superteam.

True, when Bob Howsam came to Cincinnati he had the benefit of a foundation having already been laid. The Cincinnati organization did indeed own some excellent baseball players. Bench already belonged to the Reds, the best prospect in the minor leagues. Rose was a big league star. Tony Perez was there. Even today, these three men make up the heart and soul of The Big Red Machine. But that foundation also had some cracks in it.

January 22, 1967 was the day Bob Howsam came to Cincinnati. The Reds' franchise had been declining for some time, rumors circulating everywhere that professional baseball would leave the city where it was born in 1869.

A group of business leaders joined together and

bought the team from Bill DeWitt. Their purpose was twofold. They wanted to keep a franchise in Cincinnati and they wanted to make it a success. The man they chose to run the operation as general manager was Howsam. At the time, Bob Howsam was forty-nine years old.

The son of a bee farmer in LaJara, Colorado, Howsam's career had been shaped mainly by two men. The first was the late Senator Edwin C. Johnson. Johnson was governor of Colorado for three terms, and served eighteen years in the United States Senate.

Bob Howsam married Janet Johnson, daughter of Senator Johnson. It was through Johnson, president of the Western League, that Bob Howsam entered baseball.

The Western League was one of the most successful minor leagues in the history of baseball. Howsam helped shape the league. Then came a day that changed Howsam's life. The Denver franchise became available. Howsam, his father Earl, and brother Lee, bought the club. It then was a Pittsburgh farm team, Pittsburgh being run by Branch Rickey, who is the second man who shaped Bob Howsam as a baseball man.

Denver was fighting for a pennant that year and with Howsam running the show it drew 463,000, a Class A record. It was an attendance that topped two major league clubs, the Phils and the Browns. In two other seasons Denver topped 400,000. Howsam's fame was spreading.

Time passed. William Shea of New York began organizing a third major league, the Continental League. He named as its president Branch Rickey. Rickey decided Denver would have a franchise in the league and the man who was awarded the franchise was Bob Howsam.

The Continental League was short-lived. In Congress a powerful man, Senator Edwin C. Johnson, got up and snorted about baseball's antitrust violations and unfair competition. He stirred up a hornet's nest of trouble, and rather than face an investigation, baseball gave in and expanded. But when it expanded it did so without a franchise in Denver. Bob Howsam was out of baseball.

He wasn't out of sports. The family, through their own financing, built a stadium in Denver; the stadium today being used by the minor league baseball team and the National Football League's Denver Broncos.

And born to play in that stadium was the American Football League. The founder of the Denver Broncos was Bob Howsam and family. He was, in 1960, one of the five founders of the AFL, along with Lamar Hunt, Bud Adams, Harry Wismer, and Max Winter. Soon Barron Hilton joined the group. The AFL almost bankrupted the Howsams. They did not have the money to compete. "I found," said Howsam, "I was competing with men who were in the oil business and other pursuits. I was just a farm boy." He lasted only one year. The family sold out, but not before it had made a lasting impression in the world of sports. To be sure, the Denver Broncos were an awful team but they became the most famous of the early AFL days.

The reason was the socks the team wore. Traditionally, football socks have stripes that run horizontally around the leg. Not the Denver Broncos. They were adorned with socks that ran vertically, up and down the leg. They looked, most assuredly, like clowns and often fit the role with their play.

Now Rickey was about to enter Howsam's life again. Rickey was by this time a special advisor for the St. Louis Cardinals. His special advice was to dump Bing Devine as general manager and hire Bob Howsam, an act that was accomplished on August 14, 1964. When Howsam took over as general manager the Cardinals were nine games out of first place. They won the pennant in one of the most sensational finishes in National League history, first the Phillies and then the Reds, blowing it all. As a crowning triumph the Cardinals defeated the New York Yankees, who were making their last appearance to date, in the World Series.

The following season, 1965, Bob Howsam's Cardinals finished seventh. He knew he had to make changes and that is what he did. He traded away Ken Boyer, Bill White, and Dick Groat, giving birth to his reputation as a fearless trader. The Cardinals managed to move up only to sixth the next year. But that 1966 season did prove to be a valuable one for the Cardinals. During that season Howsam traded Ray Sadecki to the San Francisco Giants for Orlando Cepeda.

In 1967 he made a stunningly successful move. He sent Charlie Smith (who?) to the New York Yankees for Roger Maris. The Cardinals again were on solid ground. What's more, he had seen attendance soar in St. Louis after the club moved into its new stadium. Attendance was at 1.7 million. So why would Bob Howsam, with success assured in St. Louis, move to Cincinnati, a team that finished seventh and drew only 743,000 fans?

"In Cincinnati," he said, "I had complete control."

There was something else. Rickey was gone at St. Louis and, to be honest, Howsam had outlived his welcome. Bob Howsam signed a three-year contract with the Cincinnati Reds. He was selected, according to the owners, because he had four qualifications.

The first was experience, something the businessmen-owners of the team totally lacked. He was promotion-minded, a man dedicated to making baseball exciting, interesting, and a family occasion. He was a great believer in building an extensive farm system, something he learned from Rickey who was the inventor of the farm system. And finally, he had experience moving into a new stadium, something that was in the works in Cincinnati.

When Bob Howsam came to Cincinnati, while he found a foundation that included Rose, Bench, and Perez — along with Lee May and Tommy Helms and others — he also found problems.

The Cincinnati organization had deteriorated badly. The minor league system was only a shell of what it should have been; some good players, true, but not being instructed well. The scouting system and front office staff were the smallest in the major leagues except for Kansas City, which had Charles O. Finley and needed no one else.

Bob Howsam came to a city that was steeped in baseball tradition and that looked upon itself as a small town. He immediately made enemies, slashing away at the people who once made up the Cincinnati Reds.

"I think when you build an organization that is to be expected," he said. "You have to make changes. You have to get people who are loyal, who have ability and are willing to carry out the goals of your organization. If a person isn't loyal I have no use for him."

Bob Howsam took a serious approach to the game he was in and to the team he was running.

"If," he says, "I've had any success in my career it's because I've tried to approach baseball from purely a business standpoint. Baseball is a business — big business."

He recalls his first day with the Reds, the thoughts of the work ahead of him.

"When I came in 1967, I had to start preparing to move into the new stadium. There were things that had to be done. I wanted to enlarge our scouting staff, set up more departments within the front office to handle group sales, promotion, public relations, tickets—even a speaker's bureau.

"But I knew this couldn't be done at one time without a large input of additional dollars. And just having come here I didn't want to ask ownership for more money.

"So I set as my first goal increased attendance, because with more attendance I would be better able to finance my other goals."

Bob Howsam went about making baseball fun in Cincinnati. But baseball can never be fun if a team doesn't win. And as successful as he'd been financially, he's been more successful in building a winning, interesting team—The Big Red Machine.

If there is one emotion Bob Howsam doesn't have it is fear. He will try anything once to see if it works. And he's tried some weird things. In Denver he inquired of scientists if it were possible to produce the aroma of a bakery, knowing the pleasant feeling one gets passing a bakery, fragrant with freshly-baked bread. He was told no.

He once commissioned a Chicago meat packer to invent an improved hot dog, getting an all-beef wiener of the best quality. The trouble was the fans preferred the old ball park hot dog. He switched back.

He suited his Denver team at one time in a "strike zone" uniform, every player's strike zone a different color from the rest of the uniform. It gave the players an eerie look, elongated, almost as if standing in front of a fun house mirror.

"Boy, did we take a razzing," Howsam recalls. "But—do you know—our hitting improved."

Fearless. He will try anything. And so it was that he created The Big Red Machine.

With his increased scouting system he signed player

after player. Don Gullett. Dave Concepcion. Ross Grimsley. Will McEnaney. Rawly Eastwick. He was building for the future. But, for the future, you must wait and Howsam wanted a winner now. So he also traded. Oh, did he trade. Secure that his people were giving him the right information and with his history of having brought Roger Maris and Orlando Cepeda to St. Louis, he went about shuffling players as if he were playing the old shell game.

On October 10, 1967 he made his first trade, sending long-time favorite Deron Johnson to Atlanta for Jim Beauchamp, Mack Jones, and Jay Ritchie. A month later he dealt another favorite, Art Shamsky. Then Tommy Harper went.

He was stripping the team clean. In January of 1968 it was Sammy Ellis, once a twenty-game winner, who was traded. Next it was Dick Simpson. Then it was John Edwards.

When the 1968 Reds took the field they were a totally different team. And there was more to come. He pulled off a shocker on June 11, 1968, obtaining pitchers Clay Carroll and Tony Cloninger, and shortstop Woody Woodward from Atlanta for Milt Pappas, Ted Davidson, and Bob Johnson.

Pappas had come to the Reds in the trade engineered by Bill DeWitt that sent Frank Robinson, labeled "an old thirty" by the team owner, to Baltimore. It was to be, perhaps, the worst trade in baseball history, Robinson winning the triple crown, the Most Valuable Player award, and leading the Orioles to a four-game sweep of Sandy Koufax and the Los Angeles Dodgers in the World Series.

Now, Howsam had salvaged that deal, getting three usable players for Pappas. Carroll, of course, became a star in the bull pen and owns the Cincinnati record of most appearances by a pitcher. Woodward, before a premature retirement, shortstopped the Reds in a World Series. And Cloninger was the workhorse of a pitching staff that was riddled with sore arms.

Howsam wasn't through. In the winter of 1968 he traded Vada Pinson, a superstar, to St. Louis for relief pitcher Wayne Granger and outfielder Bobby Tolan, an unproved talent. He was greatly criticized for the deal. Granger wound up pitching a record ninety games that year and Tolan blossomed into a star. Jim Merritt came from Minnesota for shortstop Leo Cardenas, another lifetime Red, and won twenty games.

The Big Red Machine was now born. In 1969 it was in the pennant race until the final week. The team was ready to break loose. It now had Carroll and Granger to come out of the bull pen. It had Merritt about to win his twenty games. Tolan added a dimension of speed. Woodward could handle shortstop. Lee May was at first base, Perez at third, Helms at second. Rose was in the outfield, Bench behind the plate.

Fearlessly, Howsam gambled again. He fired Dave Bristol, bringing unknown Sparky Anderson in to run the Reds in 1970.

There was an uproar. Howsam stood firm and laughed as the Machine rolled to the Western Division title, the pennant, and into a World Series it would lose. The move into Riverfront Stadium was completed and attendance records were set.

But disaster lay ahead. In 1971, crippled by injuries, the Reds slipped into a fourth-place tie. Bob Howsam knew something had to be done and he was not afraid to do it.

The Big Red Machine as it is known today was about to be recreated. The ball club Howsam had at the time was molded for old Crosley Field, a friendly little ball yard with a menacing terraced outfield and inviting fences. It was a

The Big Red Machine (left to right): Ken Griffey, Pete Rose, Don Gullett, Johnny Bench, George Foster, Joe Morgan, Cesar Geronimo, Davey Concepcion and Tony Perez.—*Fred Straub, Cincinnati Enquirer Photo*

Pete Rose's move to third base inspired The Big Red Machine but learning to play the new position was sometimes a little more than Rose asked for.
—*Wide World Photos (A & B)*

Pete Rose, the People's Choice in Cincinnati, is cooperative with young fans who want his signature.—*Fred Straub, Cincinnati Enquirer Photo*

A familiar sight in the National League playoffs, Joe Morgan sliding safely under the Pittsburgh Pirates' Rennie Stennett with a steal of second base.
—Fred Straub, Cincinnati Enquirer Photo

Sparky Anderson, alias Captain Hook, goes to the mound to remove pitcher Jack Billingham, something he did for 45 straight games to establish a major league record.—*Bob Lynn, Cincinnati Enquirer Photo*

Gary Matthews of San Francisco collides at the plate with Johnny Bench, causing a shoulder injury that plagued Bench throughout the 1975 season.—*Wide World Photos*

Johnny Bench and Vickie Chesser exchange vows in the wedding of the year in Cincinnati, one day before the opening of Spring training.
—*Bob Lynn, Cincinnati Enquirer Photo*

The scoreboard at Riverfront Stadium calls Tony Perez ''The RBI King,'' which he has just become with the 1000th run batted in of his career. At left he stands at first base with San Diego's Mike Ivie. At upper right his children, Victor (l) and Eduardo receive the historic ball while the fans give Perez a standing ovation.—*Terry Armor, Cincinnati Post Photo*

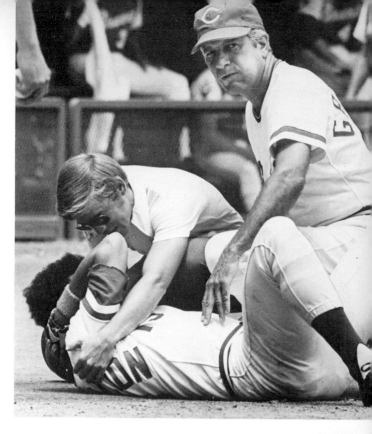

It was a rough year for Dave Concepcion. He is attended to on the ground by trainer Larry Starr as Alex Grammas leers at Atlanta pitcher Mike Beard. Beard and Concepcion collided, knocking Concepcion down. In other photo Starr attends to Concepcion as Grammas (l) and Sparky Anderson look on. Concepcion suffered a broken bone in his wrist when hit by a pitch from Dale Murray of Montreal.
—*Fred Straub and Bob Free, Cincinnati Enquirer Photos*

THAT HIT BY PETE ROSE
/AS THE 2,500TH OF HIS
MAJOR LEAGUE CAREER
HE'S THE 52ND PLAYER
IN HISTORY TO REACH
THE 2,500 MARK

Umpire John McSherry presents Pete Rose
with the ball used when Rose recorded the
2500th hit of his career as the scoreboard
tells the story in lights at Riverfront Stadium.
—*Terry Armor, Cincinnati Post Photo*

Ken Griffey takes a moment out of
spring training to sign an
autograph for a young Reds' rooter.
—*Fred Straub, Cincinnati Enquirer Photo*

park that begged for power. The Reds had power—Bench, Perez and May—in the middle of the lineup. But they were all right-handed and the team was susceptible to right-handed pitching.

What's more, in Riverfront Stadium on AstroTurf, speed was a requirement. Bob Howsam was a speed man, having studied at the knee of Rickey. His minor league system did not yet have the players ready to fill the Reds' needs. Howsam had to go outside to get it.

He studied reports from his people. He held meetings.

"For the last six weeks of the season," recalled Sparky Anderson, "I was scouting the other teams as much as I was managing."

At this same time there were things happening in Houston that were to lead to the trade of trades. The Astros had finished in a fourth-place tie with the Reds. Harry Walker was manager of the Astros. He was convinced of one thing. He was one hitter short of being a contender.

"Get me a power hitter, someone who can hit fourth and hit the long ball," Walker instructed his front office. The front office balked. At that time the Astros had a kid who they felt was going to be one of the great power hitters in the game. His name was John Mayberry. Everyone in the front office liked Mayberry. Walker didn't and the feeling was mutual. Harry Walker had tried to make Mayberry hit the ball to the opposite field. Mayberry didn't like that. He idolized Willie McCovey. He was 6-foot-3 and strong.

There was a definite split between Walker and Mayberry. Not that this was unusual. There was a split between Walker and most of his players. He and Joe Morgan couldn't get along, Walker blaming Morgan for being a bad influence on Jimmy Wynn. And Bob Watson and Walker had their troubles. Walker wanted Watson to stop pulling the baseball. It went to the extreme.

Walker approached Bob Watson one day. He pointed at the 390-foot sign in left center. "See that sign," said Walker. "The next time you hit a ball to the left of it it's gonna cost you fifty dollars. The time after that, it's gonna cost you a hundred dollars. And the time after that, I'm sending you to Oklahoma City."

Watson hit one ball to left field. It cost him fifty dollars. Two days later he hit another to left field. It cost him a hundred dollars. Then he hit a third ball to left. He was shipped to Oklahoma City where he hit about .400 for two weeks before being recalled. When that happened the word got back to general manager Spec Richardson of the Astros. He instructed Walker to leave Watson alone as a hitter. He is now the best hitter Houston has.

Walker's split with the players, though, was vital in the anatomy of the deal that was to come about. He demanded a power hitter. "Get me the man Harry wants," Spec Richardson said finally to his staff.

Grady Hatton, a former Houston manager, was instructed to go out and find the person Walker wanted. So Hatton was scouting the big leagues for a power hitter while the Reds had Ray Shore, their super scout, out scouting the big leagues for someone who could add speed to the team, an outfielder who could patrol the spacious centerfield in Riverfront Stadium and some additional pitching.

Grady Hatton at season's end reported to Spec Richardson.

"Of all the people available who exactly fit what Harry wants, Lee May is the man," said Hatton. So Lee May it was. Houston wanted Lee May. At the same time, though, Bob Howsam's scouts were reporting back to him.

"Joe Morgan," said Ray Shore, the Reds' super scout.

"Joe Morgan," advised Alex Grammas, the Reds' third base coach and former major league infielder.

Sparky Anderson wasn't sure. "I had only seen Morgan for a couple of years. Naturally, I liked him but I wasn't ready to jump off no bridges to get him. He hadn't hit overly good against us. But I do remember one thing. He hit Don Gullett real good and Grammas told me Morgan hit Sandy Koufax real well, too."

So it was that the forces were at work to bring Spec Richardson and Bob Howsam together in the press room at the Sheraton-Palace Hotel during the National League playoffs of 1971.

They began talking. The Reds were interested in Morgan. They'd be willing to give up Lee May. Richardson said he'd think it over. They talked again in Oakland during the American League playoffs. The deal was sprouting wings. It grew almost daily, trying to even itself out. May for Morgan. That wasn't enough. Okay, Houston would put Denis Menke into the trade. They had no spot for him, Roger Metzger having taken over as shortstop.

Bob Howsam liked that. He saw Menke as the answer to the long-lingering problem at third base. Perez was, in reality a first baseman, not a third baseman. He was forced to play third to make room for Lee May who could play no other position. Now May would be gone, Perez could move to first and Menke could fill the bill defensively at third base. And it went further. Richardson said he needed Tommy Helms to replace Morgan.

Jack Billingham came into the trade. Houston thought of the tall right-hander as only a relief pitcher. They had, after all, Larry Dierker and Don Wilson. They agreed to put Billingham in the deal. Now Anderson liked the deal. "I was satisfied with it right there," he said, "and to be honest,

I was getting nervous. I wanted to complete it."

Anderson had reason to worry. Houston was also talking to the Los Angeles Dodgers.

During the World Series Anderson and Shore were in the press room when they heard a rumor. The Dodgers and Houston were about to finalize a deal—Joe Morgan for the Dodgers' smooth-fielding first baseman, Wes Parker.

"We shot out of that room and went looking for Mr. Howsam," Anderson recalls. "We looked everywhere until we finally found him and told him what we'd heard."

"Now," Howsam said, "we've got to find Spec."

So the search started again, the Reds' threesome looking for the general manager of the Houston Astros. After an hour they came across him, Anderson and Shore blending off into the background so the two executives could talk.

"Don't do anything hastily; we'll get together yet," promised Howsam. Richardson took him at his word. The Dodger deal was off.

Days turned into weeks. Richardson and Howsam conversed via long distance almost daily. Still nothing. They got together at the general managers' meetings in Jacksonville, Florida. Still nothing. A couple of times, it looked like the trade had fallen through.

Finally, Richardson asked for Jimmy Stewart, a well-liked utility player who had earned the nickname "Super Sub" while in Cincinnati. That opened the door for Howsam. Okay, he said, you can have Stewart if we can have Cesar Geronimo and another player.

Geronimo was a weak-hitting outfielder with tremendous speed and the strongest throwing arm in baseball. Although he didn't fit into the Houston plans, the Astros balked. The deal was delayed.

Why Geronimo? Because Ray Shore liked him. He saw that he had a chance to hit and that, even if he didn't, he would be a valuable asset in the vast centerfield in Riverfront Stadium.

December came along and baseball's executives headed to Phoenix, Arizona, for their annual convention. The talks continued. Houston, though, was drooling for May. They figured they filled the hole left by trading Morgan by obtaining Helms, a Gold Glove second baseman and a fine hitter. What's more, by obtaining May it would allow them to trade John Mayberry for the relief pitcher they needed.

They agreed to Geronimo and presented Howsam with a list of three players from which to select one. On the list was Keith Lampard who had hit a home run to beat the Reds in a crucial game during the stretch run in 1969. There was another player, now forgotten by all involved, and there was Ed Armbrister, an outfielder from the Bahamas.

Howsam and Shore were highest on Armbrister. They selected him. Armbrister, it turned out, would drive in the winning run in the playoff sweep over the Pittsburgh Pirates in 1975, the year when the Reds won it all.

On the morning of November 11, 1971, the Reds' group in attendance at the winter convention gathered for their daily briefing at the Camelback Inn.

"Does anyone have to make a phone call or leave the room?" said Howsam. The members of the Reds' staff looked at each other in disbelief. They had no idea what was going on. They all shook their heads no.

"This is your last chance," he said. Again they said no.

"Okay, then we're gonna stay locked up right here. We've just completed a deal with Houston and there will be no outside communication until the deal is announced," said Howsam.

Secrecy, a trademark of the Howsam organization. Into the press room sneaked the public relations director. He pinned a notice on the board. It merely said that a major trade would be announced at three p.m.

The writers in attendance thought it was a joke upon discovering the notice. It didn't mention which teams were involved, something all trade notices carry, so at least the press of those teams involved can be in attendance. But it was no joke. At three p.m. Roger Ruhl, then the public relations director of the Reds, his voice quivering as this was his first trade announcement ever, said:

"The Cincinnati Reds have just traded first baseman Lee May, second baseman Tommy Helms, and utilityman Jimmy Stewart to the Houston Astros for second baseman Joe Morgan, pitcher Jack Billingham, infielder Denis Menke, and outfielders Cesar Geronimo and Ed Armbrister."

All hell broke loose. The Creation had been completed.

Off to one side stood Grady Hatton, the man who recommended Lee May. He had some doubts. "If this deal doesn't bring us a pennant in two years, it's a bad deal," he confided. He was, however, fully confident that it would win that pennant for Houston.

Although they refused to admit it at the time, there was some concern among the Reds' people. Howsam was to admit it much later. "We were going for something in the future," he said. "I would not have been surprised — and had figured it might happen — if we had given Houston a pennant."

The deal actually worked to improve both teams. The Reds won the pennant while Houston went on to put together its best record ever in 1972.

However, it also signified the beginning of the end for

the Astros. They traded Mayberry to Kansas City, where he became one of the most feared power hitters in the American League, for relief pitcher Jim York. Said at the time to be the best relief pitcher in the American League, York wound up spending most of his days as an Astro in the minor leagues.

Other bad deals were to follow. Jimmy Wynn to the Dodgers for Claude Osteen. They traded away Mike Marshall. They traded Mike Cuellar. And there was more to the trade between the Reds and Astros. Menke filled in as the perfect third baseman for the Reds, handling the job through two Western Division titles and one pennant. By 1974, though, he was ready to give up baseball.

This story, in reality, begins in the summer of 1974 when Bob Howsam was making one of his trips back home to Denver. Over the years, Howsam had built a close relationship with Frank Harraway, a Denver baseball writer who had covered the Bears forever. It was Harraway's birthday and Howsam took the writer and his wife to lunch.

At lunch that day, Howsam began picking his friend's brain about the minor league players in Denver. He asked him if there were any prospects there.

"They have a pitcher by the name of Pat Darcy who is a fine looking prospect," said the writer. Howsam didn't give it a whole lot of thought but did, as he says, "file it in the back of my mind."

Now, with the season just about over, Menke approached Howsam and told him he didn't think he would play another year in Cincinnati. "If you could place me back in Houston so I could be where my business interests are, I would play another year," said Menke.

Howsam promised to make an effort. He called Richardson and explained the Menke situation. "We'd be interested in having him," said Richardson. "He'd make a fine utility player for us."

"Fine then," answered Howsam. "Get together a list of players you feel will be available for Menke and keep in mind I'd like a young player with the potential of having some ability."

When the list was delivered, on it was the name Darcy. A light went on in Howsam's mind. He began checking with his scouts on Darcy and got encouragement so he made the deal. A year later, as The Big Red Machine marched to glory, rookie pitcher Pat Darcy won ten and lost five.

So it was that the deal was even more of a blessing for the Reds than it seemed back there in the winter of 1971. However, there was much irony involved in the Creation. In Houston the public rejoiced in the trade. They had obtained Lee May, one of the great power hitters in the game, and Helms, an All-Star second baseman. In Cincinnati it met with disdain. Howsam had dared trade away two of the most popular players ever to wear a Cincinnati uniform. He had traded away two of the team's most visible leaders. Had he destroyed the team?

The press greeted the deal as if it had just found a rattlesnake between the sheets. Bob Howsam was publicly chastised as he never had been before.

The man in the street reacted violently.

"It looks like a lousy deal to me. What'd they get in the trade? They probably thought May would be up for a raise this year since he had his best season," said one fan.

"Somebody must have hypnotized Howsam," said another.

"The trade is just idiotic," added a third. "Any one of the three for the whole Houston team would have been a good trade."

And a Mt. Adams artist—Mt. Adams being a bohemian section of Cincinnati—added: "The best trade would have been Sparky Anderson and Bob Howsam for a comedy team, preferably one with a trained seal."

But Howsam remained confident. He had done his homework. He knew what he had given up and he knew what he had gotten. He resented the criticism, his track record having shown nothing but success in ball player transactions.

During spring training he said to a highly critical writer in the most sarcastic of fashions, "We'll show you what you know about trading."

He was right. By 1975 all five of the players obtained from Houston—Morgan, Billingham, Geronimo, Armbrister, and Darcy—were key members of the Reds.

Meanwhile, in Houston Menke and Stewart had retired. Helms was parked on the bench, unable to get along with Preston Gomez who was to be fired as manager, and May was in Baltimore having been traded for two players who did little to help the Astros. As the Reds won the pennant, Houston finished last and Spec Richardson was fired.

By this time Howsam had moved from general manager to president of the Reds, having gained the title on March 20, 1973.

His debut as president began in the most auspicious of manners. He was in Tampa, Florida at spring training, the newly-named president of the Reds, talking outside the press room when a fan approached him.

"Say, buddy," said the fan, "where's the men's room?"

His first official act was showing the fan where the men's room was.

The Houston trade laid the groundwork, but there was more to do, and totally free as president of the club, Howsam did it. His farm system now was developing ball players. Dave Concepcion had come of age and was an All-Star shortstop. George Foster, obtained in 1971 from the San Francisco Giants, for shortstop Frank Duffy and Vern Geishert, a pitcher who quickly retired, was given a chance to play and became the talk of the National League.

All the while fans flocked to Riverfront Stadium and parks around the league to see The Big Red Machine. More than two million have come to Riverfront Stadium for three years straight, a feat that defies explanation in one of the league's smallest communities.

Profits soared. Ownership was happy. The city was happy. The players were happy. And the Creation goes on. Howsam keeps signing players for the future, believing in a farm system as the lifeblood of an organization. He keeps looking for trades that will help his team, hoping for another Morgan or Foster.

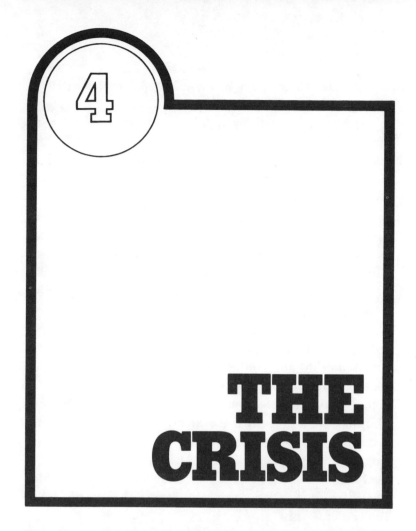

THE CRISIS

The winter of 1974 was not a happy one for Tony Perez. A skinny kid who spoke no English, he had left his native Cuba in 1960 to play baseball as a professional. The team that scouted him and signed him was the Cincinnati Reds.

He had climbed through the minor leagues as part of the Cincinnati organization. He had come to the big leagues and been a star, if an underrated one. He had sacrificed for the good of the team. A first baseman, he had moved to third base to make room for power-hitting Lee May and become an adequate infielder. Then, when May was traded in 1972, he returned to first base.

Tony Perez had been the picture of consistency for the Cincinnati Reds, their most feared hitter in the clutch. And now, after fourteen seasons in the Cincinnati organization, ten of them with the big league Reds, he spent the winter worrying what the future was to hold.

Late in the 1974 season when it had become obvious that the Reds would not catch Los Angeles and would finish no better than second, Bob Howsam had called Perez to his plush office on the third floor of Riverfront Stadium.

The Reds had spent much time analyzing their personnel and had reached one conclusion. Danny Driessen, who had played third base throughout 1974, could not return as a third baseman in 1975. A splendid hitter, Driessen could not handle the defensive end of third base. He was a natural first baseman, the man the Reds thought of as their future first baseman. The future seemed to be now. The Reds needed a third baseman. They knew that Tony Perez was thirty-two years old. He couldn't go on much longer. He was replaceable with Driessen. If they could get the front-line third baseman they needed — a good fielder who hit right-handed and with power — they would trade Tony Perez for him.

There was a catch. Tony Perez was protected by the new five- and ten-year rule which stated that a player who had played ten years in the major leagues, the last five with the same club, could not be traded without his permission. So it was that Bob Howsam beckoned Tony Perez to his office late in the season of 1974.

"Tony," said Howsam, "I'm not saying we're going to trade you. I don't know what we are going to do this winter. But I'd like to have you sign a waiver of the five- and ten-year rule so that we can trade you if the right deal comes along."

Tony Perez balked. Not that he would have caused trouble. Tony Perez is the sweetest person on earth and the chances are he would have made no trouble for anyone. But he wasn't going to sign the piece of paper.

"I want to go to a contender if you trade me," argued Perez. "I don't want to go to a bad club."

Howsam pressed on. He could not make that promise. He explained to Perez that he could be the difference between a club being a good club or a bad club. That he, Tony Perez, could make a winner out of a loser. Tony Perez said no thank you. He refused to sign the waiver. Instead he went home to sit on the beach in San Juan, Puerto Rico, where the temperature was eighty-five, and wait for the phone to ring, to hear where he had been traded. The rumors were flying everywhere. Perez to Boston, with The Green Monster beckoning in left field, for Roger Moret. Perez to Oakland for Sal Bando. Perez to Kansas City for George Brett or Pete Mackanin. Perez to the New York Yankees for Graig Nettles.

All the deals fell through. When baseball's winter convention ended in New Orleans, Tony Perez was still a member of the Cincinnati Reds. It was to prove that sometimes the best deals are the ones you don't make.

Meanwhile, in Puerto Rico Danny Driessen was breaking his wrist on a tag play at first base. Suddenly, Perez wasn't quite so available. To fill the third base gap, at least defensively, Bob Howsam went out and got the best man he could find, John Vukovich, a defensive wizard who could neither hit nor run.

The winter dragged on. Contracts were sent out. They, on the whole, reflected the Reds' inability to catch the

Dodgers. But none reflected the stand of management any stronger than the contract sent to Pete Rose. He was in a state of shock when he opened his mail and saw that the club's original offer was calling for a pay cut of nearly twenty percent, the maximum allowed. It was true that for the first time in a decade Pete Rose had failed to hit .300, falling off to .284. But in Pete Rose's eyes, he had not had "a bad year."

"I did the things I'm supposed to do," he argued. "In fact I did them better than anyone else in the world. I'm paid to get on base, score runs, be a leader. I did all that." He did lead the league in doubles with forty-five, in runs scored with 110. He did play every one of the team's 163 games. He did draw 106 walks, a career high. He made just one error on defense. He did all that and they were offering him a huge pay cut and telling him he was too fat, that he had to lose weight.

"I miss .300 for the first time in ten years and suddenly I'm out of shape and a 'fat boy,'" moaned Rose.

Three weeks went by. Rose was getting nowhere. Twice he had walked out on negotiations, infuriated. Finally, on February 7 Pete Rose signed his thirteenth contract with the Cincinnati Reds. He had avoided outside arbitration even though he believed he would have won. He said he was happy with the contract but that was untrue. To bring peace to the team and to himself, he had accepted a three percent pay cut, which is a big hunk of cash when you are making $160,000 a year.

It was now time for spring training, Sparky Anderson's sixth as manager of The Big Red Machine. He had questions that had to be answered and answered quickly: Would Gary Nolan come back? Was John Vukovich the answer at third base? Was Rose ready to hit .300 again?

Could Ken Griffey do the job in right field? What could he do with Driessen?

All this and it was vital that the team get off to a fast start, seven games in the first two weeks of the season being against the Los Angeles Dodgers. A slow start, which had become a Cincinnati tradition, could end the pennant race almost before it started.

No fewer than seven players showed up to contend for the third base job. Nolan came on slowly. Griffey seemed ready. Rose was eager. Camp went smoothly. Tony Perez and Johnny Bench were hitting baseballs all over Florida, Perez going so far as to state "you may not be wrong if you vote for me for Most Valuable Player this year."

A week before the season was to open Vukovich was named the third baseman. And Sparky Anderson cut his roster. Among the cuts was a young right-handed relief pitcher named Rawly Eastwick. Anderson said that "Eastwick was the toughest one for me to cut." Eastwick would return, just as Vukovich would disappear. Spring training had come to an end. Perez had hit .450. Bench had hit .436. They were ready for opening day.

Opening day in Cincinnati is something out of the ordinary. It is a holiday, a cause for a gala celebration. The schools let students with tickets attend the game. There are parades. The politicians who will not again be seen until playoff time come out from hiding.

This, though, was to be a special opening day. The Dodgers were in town, the hated Dodgers. The Reds thought about the Dodgers, about this series, about getting off quickly.

"I wouldn't mind if we were playing them eighteen straight to open the season. This just gets us down to business earlier. I want no breaks. Just let's get down to head-to-head baseball and see who is best," said Sparky Anderson.

He was anxious. His team was anxious. It was a new year. The year of The Big Red Machine.

There were 52,526 jamming Riverfront Stadium. They got more than a baseball game. They got a war. It went fourteen innings and the Reds came out on top 2-1, in a storm of controversy.

It ended as George Foster, the fourth man in the Reds' three-man outfield, beat out a roller to third baseman Ron Cey, Cesar Geronimo coming across the plate with the winning run. The play at first was close, so close, but the safe call was given by Umpire Paul Pryor and it was over.

"In my heart," said Steve Garvey, the Dodger first baseman, and Most Valuable Player the year before, "I knew we had him."

All Foster could say was, "It was a split-second play. I could have been called safe or out. But I go along with the umpire."

The Dodgers, so calm a year earlier as they won the pennant, now were steaming. This wasn't one game they had lost, this was the start of a trend and they seemed to sense it. They ranted and they raved and they cursed the umpire. It was a stark contrast to the team of a year ago, so sure of itself, so cocky and imperturbable.

Joe Morgan sat at his locker in the winning clubhouse and added fuel to the fire. "They can't think they're better than us."

Game Number 2 was to be more of the same. The Dodgers led 3-2, entering the bottom of the ninth inning. Mike Marshall was on the mound for the Dodgers, the same Mike Marshall who a year earlier had been quoted as saying "pitching against the Reds is like pitching against a bunch of high school kids."

Mike Marshall was to lose. Ken Griffey led off with a triple, surviving a Dodger appeal that he missed second base. Darrel Chaney then lashed a hit to right and then was bunted to second by rookie Doug Flynn, making his first big league appearance.

Sparky Anderson now was ready to hit for Pedro Borbon, his third pitcher in the game. He could choose between Foster, the first-game hero, or Davey Concepcion who had suffered a pulled muscle in the opener and was on the bench.

He picked Concepcion, his first of many brilliant decisions during the season. Concepcion, who had sat in the Reds' sauna during the game to get warm, came on and blooped a hit to center. Victory for the Reds.

Game Number 3: down 5-0 and then victory. Tony Perez, the self-proclaimed MVP of the spring, but off to an 0-for-13 start, came up in the bottom of the eighth inning and slammed a double into the left-field corner. Rose raced home with the run that produced a 7-6 Cincinnati victory.

Three wins all by one run over the Dodgers. "That," shouted Perez, "is how they beat us last year. Now we have won three one-run games, two coming from behind. It is a new year."

But things were to turn bad and the turn was to come in a big hurry. First in San Diego where there were two losses in three games. Then it was on to Los Angeles to meet the Dodgers again, this time in a four-game series, a series the Dodgers were to sweep.

In the first game it was Marshall taunting and teasing Bench and Perez as he worked out of trouble to get a save. In the second game it was Don Sutton overpowering Cincinnati with a one-hitter, the hit being a Johnny Bench home run. But it was in the third game of the series that Cincinnati's troubles became visible. In the second inning with the game scoreless Sparky Anderson sent Danny Driessen to the plate to hit for a flabbergasted John Vukovich. In the second inning! Vukovich threw a temper tantrum. Anderson didn't care. The writing was on the wall. John Vukovich would not remain Cincinnati's third baseman for very long.

The next night, with Driessen just three days off the disabled list at first base, the Dodgers won again. They won when Driessen let a ground ball hit by Willie Crawford go right between his legs as if he were a croquet wicket. Jimmy Wynn raced home from second base with the run that gave Los Angeles a 5-4 victory.

The crisis had begun.

When the Reds won it was usually a miracle win. Like Sunday, April 20. They were trailing Houston 7-1 in the fifth inning. They were to win 9-8, and do it because Concepcion stole a base while six runs behind. The Reds were showing that they would run no matter what the situation, no matter what the score.

"You have to keep playing your game," explained Anderson. "If you don't, you might as well fold up your tent." But as often as the Reds won, they lost. They lost one game when Flynn lost a high bouncing ground ball in the stadium lights. "Crazy," sobbed Anderson. "Damn, we've lost some tough games."

As April ended the Reds stood just 12-11. Since sweeping the Dodgers in the opening series they had won but nine games. They were three games behind Los Angeles. Pete Rose was moved to third base and John Vukovich sent packing. Rawly Eastwick was recalled from the minor leagues to help in the bull pen.

There was a brief spurt, the Reds jumping to 18-13 on May 11. Tom Seaver was pitching that day for the Mets and Pete Rose led off the game with a home run. The Reds wound up losing 3-2.

As the Reds came to Philadelphia for a four-game series Anderson decided it was time to hold a clubhouse meeting. As a team the Reds are a jolly bunch, but they get their jollies by ripping one another's abilities. "It is," explains Joe Morgan, "our way of staying loose."

Anderson, though, detected a fear among some of his younger players. He called it "Indianapolis fever," the fear of being returned to the minor leagues with the team going at less than full speed ahead. So he imposed a gag rule on the Reds. There was to be no more ripping. The effort was to relax the youngsters, kids who didn't quite know what to make of it when Rose, Perez, and Morgan got to ripping everything — including them — in sight.

Philadelphia came and went. Four straight losses. On to Montreal. Another loss and a damaging one, Tony Scott sliding hard into Morgan at second base. Morgan didn't realize it right away but his shin had been split open.

"It was ugly," recalled Rose. "You could see clear down to the bone." Fourteen stitches were applied to Joe Morgan's shin. No one knew when he would play again. And The Big Red Machine was getting tighter and tighter. They had lost six in a row. They stood at 18-19. The Dodgers had opened up a five and a half game lead. Up until this moment the Reds had wandered lost through the National League. Perez was not hitting. The lineup wasn't stable. Bench had not driven in runs. The pitching was inconsistent. The team had made a multitude of baserunning and fielding blunders. And there was no life in the clubhouse, Anderson's gag rule leaving his team with no way to let off steam.

May 19 dawned. The Reds were all sitting around the clubhouse in Montreal quietly, no one daring to say anything off line to anyone else.

Enter Joe Morgan. He had just come from the doctor's

office. He had had enough of the losing. After all, had he not said opening day about the Dodgers that "they can't think they're better than us."

He burst into the clubhouse, a wide smile on his face. "Screw you, Perez. Screw you, Rose. Screw you, Bench. And that goes for you, too," he shouted. He was pointing at Anderson. Anderson's face, at first dour, broke into a smile. The clubhouse rocked with laughter.

"When you gonna hit a home run, Perez?" Morgan began.

"When you gonna play again? That little scratch on your leg gonna keep you out of the lineup for a month, eh?" answered Perez.

"I'm playing today," said Morgan.

And play he did with the fourteen stitches. Bench with a fever and a sore throat played even though he wasn't expected to. The losing streak came to an end with Griffey and Bench hitting tenth-inning home runs to win it. It was Bench's first run batted in since May 7.

The Reds were off and running.

"That right there, when Morgan came into the clubhouse and began shouting, that was the turning point," said Anderson. "We came back to life."

If that was the turning point, the inspiration was to come four days later. The Reds were at .500, winning twenty and losing twenty. They were going against Tom Seaver and had spotted him a 3-0 lead. But "Tom Terrific" was not to win this one. Before the fourth inning was over he was out of the game, Perez having tied the game with a three-run homer and the Reds adding four unearned runs the next inning.

"Maybe," said Sparky Anderson, "this is a sign things are turning around."

The Winning Streak

On May 2, 1975 the Cincinnati Reds lost a 6-5 decision to the Atlanta Braves, blowing a 5-2 lead on a three-run pinch-hit home run by Clarence Gaston and then a ninth-inning, solo home run by Larvell Blanks. Down by a run in the bottom of the ninth inning that day, the Reds put runners at first and second with one out. The 21,061 gathered expected another miracle finish.

But it wasn't to be, Joe Morgan failing with a fly ball to centerfield and Johnny Bench hitting into a game-ending force. With the loss the Reds' record for the season dropped to 12-12.

"We're not a .500 club," moaned Sparky Anderson in a quiet Cincinnati dressing room.

Indeed the Reds weren't. But for the want of a hit in a key situation they would have been lavishing in first place. Eight of their twelve losses had come by a scant run and two others by only two runs. The hitting, though, just wasn't there. Tony Perez was batting a pauperly .187. Johnny Bench was hitting .250. Each owned nineteen runs batted in, respectable enough for twenty-four games, but not when the opportunities they had been presented with are considered.

In the first twenty-four games Bench had batted with sixty-one runners in scoring position, Perez with fifty-nine. Bench had come to bat with 102 runners on base, Perez with ninety. The RBI totals were misleading. The major deficiency, though, was that Cincinnati lacked a third baseman. Over the winter they had acquired John Vukovich, owner of a .154 lifetime batting average. The thinking was that Vukovich performed artfully in the field, and with the Reds' heavy artillery up front they could carry a weak bat.

Anderson was soon to learn he couldn't carry Vukovich's bat. It reached a climax in the season's ninth game, another one-run loss, this one to the hated Dodgers.

Vukovich was the scheduled hitter with the bases loaded, one out, in the *second inning*. At this point Anderson made his move. He pinch-hit for Vukovich even though the game was still scoreless. Vukovich threw a temper tantrum much to Anderson's dislike. Sparky refused to explain his move to Vukovich.

"Who would you rather see hitting with the bases loaded," was all he would say. "Vukovich or Danny Driessen?" Vukovich did not play much third base after that. The position was split by the rookie Doug Flynn, and the veteran Darrel Chaney. Each fielded well. Neither hit. Something had to be done and that brings us back to May 2 and that loss to the Atlanta Braves. Sparky Anderson had a brainstorm.

It was early on the dreary evening, the Cincinnati Reds taking batting practice. Sparky Anderson emerged from the long tunnel that leads from the dugout through the bowels of Riverfront Stadium back to the Reds' locker room. He looked at first base and standing there taking throws from Darrel Chaney was Pete Rose. He was wearing a first baseman's glove, a new one he had gotten for his daughter Fawn. He was breaking the glove in so she could use it when she played softball.

Anderson approached Rose. "I wish you were over there," said Sparky.

"Over where?" asked Rose.

"There," said Anderson, pointing toward third base.

"Third base?" pressed Rose.

"Yep," said Anderson.

"You want me to play there?" an unbelieving Rose said.

"Yep," said Anderson.

"When?" inquired Rose.

"Tomorrow too soon?" said Anderson.

Pete Rose said "Okay," and hustled off to the locker room for an infielder's glove and a protective cup. On returning, he started taking ground balls at third base one after another for forty-five minutes.

The following day was Kentucky Derby Day, May 3. It was raining. Batting practice had been cancelled. Only one player was on the field for any type of pregame practice.

Pete Rose, a $160,000-a-year superstar, was standing at third base with the tarpaulin rolled back so he could perform, taking ground balls. For forty-five minutes Alex Grammas hit them and for forty-five minutes Pete Rose made the plays.

He was about to debut as a third baseman.

And what a debut it was! Ralph Garr, the speedy Atlanta lead-off hitter and the defending National League batting champion, was the first batter and he tested Rose right away with a tricky grounder that led to a tough throw.

"Out," shouted Bob Engel, the first base umpire. Pete Rose had arrived.

"I thought about moving him there all spring," admitted Anderson, "but I didn't think he would take too kindly to the idea."

When you have been a Most Valuable Player, a three-time batting champion, having given thirteen years to one team and are the team captain, to say nothing of being a one-time Gold Glove outfielder, you normally have gained enough stature so that the manager will ask you before he makes a radical move involving you. Rose had reached that point in his career. What's more, Anderson knew the history of Pete Rose at third base.

In 1966 Don Heffner was named manager of the Reds in a move that was to be proved one of the worst decisions ever made by a baseball executive. The first thing Heffner did was announce Pete Rose was going to be his third baseman. Two years earlier, Rose had won Rookie of the Year honors as a second baseman. That was his position, he felt.

"I was coming off my first really good year," recalled Rose. "I'd just hit .300 for the first time. I didn't want to move then. I did something I've never done before or since. I sulked. I moped around all spring training. I didn't get ready."

The trial of Pete Rose at third base in 1966 was a disaster as was the short-lived term as manager of Don Heffner. Rose lasted all of sixteen games at third base, hitting a miserable .187. In the end, Heffner gave in. He moved Rose back to second and almost immediately his average shot back over the .300 mark. In midseason Heffner was fired and from that point on everyone believed that Pete Rose didn't want to play third base.

"I was young then," says Rose. "I'm more mature now. I realize if it will help the team, I will do it." The attitude of the man they call "Charlie Hustle" was never better illustrated. He has through the years been called a selfish player because he worries about hitting .300 and getting 200 hits. His critics call those personal goals.

"Those are team goals," challenges Rose. "If I hit .300 and get 200 hits as a lead-off man it means I'm on base. That means I'm scoring runs and runs are what win ball games."

Consider, if you will, what sacrifice Rose really made. He was, at age thirty-four, going to a brand new position strictly on an experimental basis. He had been secure in the outfield, a position that is easy on the legs and that allows you time to think between at-bats. He was taking a chance of embarrassing himself at a position he once had failed at. Yet he agreed, to help the team.

"If he had embarrassed himself or if his hitting had fallen off I'd have taken him off third," says Sparky Anderson. "After the thirteen years he's given the Reds I'm not about to make him embarrass himself. He's too great a player."

Rose was an instant success at third base.

"I'm like a kid with a new toy. It's like being reborn," he said.

And he played like it. He went all the way until May 21 before making his first error on a slow roller hit by Tom Seaver of the Mets. The play was so close, so controversial, that Mets' coach, Joe Pignatano, disagreeing with the official scorer, waved a white towel at the press box while Rose and his teammates begged for a change in the ruling.

"I don't mind making errors," said Rose. "But this was my first one and it was a bad call." Such is the pride of the man who is Pete Rose. Pride was the reason he succeeded at third base, pride in himself and in his team.

With Rose at third the Reds suddenly had the highest paid infield in baseball history. Perez was making an estimated $100,000 at first; Joe Morgan an estimated $132,000 at second; Dave Concepcion an estimated $65,000 at short; Rose an estimated $158,000 at third; and Bench an estimated $170,000 catching.

With Rose at third the Reds immediately took off on a four-game winning streak and went on to win six of their next seven. But there was one more 1975 lull to come—in the form of a six-game losing streak.

On May 16 they dropped a 4-2 decision to Montreal,

their record falling to 18-19. It was the last day in 1975 that The Big Red Machine was to be below .500.

Rose's move to third opened a spot in the outfield, a spot for a much-needed bat. The bat was needed because Bench still was having trouble driving in runs. When he followed a Ken Griffey homer on May 17 with one of his own, it was his first run batted in since May 7, ten long days. The man who benefitted most from Rose's switch was George Foster, who was to blossom into star status and give the Reds the most devastating lineup in baseball.

Suddenly there were no more "outs" in the Red attack. The first eight men could hit and were to do so all season. The losing streak ended when Griffey and Bench homered in the tenth inning at Montreal. The next day Rose and Foster each homered in a victory. After a loss in New York the Reds rolled off seven straight. And while the Reds were winning the Dodgers were losing. The gap was sliced to a game and a half by the seven-game streak, longest winning skein the Reds had produced in three years.

Sparky Anderson, through a brainstorm that he never had a chance of revealing even to club president Bob Howsam, had found the missing link. He had come up with the key to open the door to success.

The infield was solid and so was the outfield—Foster in left, Cesar Geronimo in center, and Ken Griffey in right. A bargain basement outfield behind the million-dollar infield. Each member of the outfield complemented the other. Griffey's forte was speed. Foster's was power. Geronimo's was defense. Each was quiet. Each was a late bloomer. And each came to the Reds for virtually nothing.

Geronimo, as previously discussed, came in the great Houston holdup that led to the Creation. He had shown nothing when with the Astros but there was a reason.

Geronimo's baseball background was lacking. He grew up in El Seibo, Dominican Republic. His early years weren't spent playing baseball, they were spent at Santo Tomas De Aquino, a seminary. Geronimo was studying for the priesthood.

While he studied, though, he dreamed . . . dreamed of baseball. After lights out at the seminary when everyone was tucked neatly away in bed Geronimo would lie with a portable radio under his pillow.

"I always listen to the winter league games in the bedroom after the others fall asleep," he said. For five years he studied for the priesthood, all the while dreaming of baseball. From the time he was twelve years old until he was seventeen he remained at Santo Tomas De Aquino, never truly fulfilled. He had to get out and he did.

Geronimo did not step right into baseball. The best he could do was wind up as a centerfielder for a softball team sponsored by Casino Cigarettes, a long way from the big time. One afternoon Geronimo's father approached him. He had read in the newspaper that the New York Yankees were holding a tryout camp in El Seibo. The elder Geronimo loaded his son into the car and off they went to join more than one hundred hopefuls at the camp. Cesar Geronimo had never played for a team that used a baseball. His assets were speed and an unbelievable throwing arm.

Pepe Seda was the Yankee scout on hand and he was impressed with the raw talent he saw. He asked Geronimo to return the next day. What a surprise Geronimo had when Seda told him to walk up on that funny hill in the middle of the diamond and try to throw a baseball over home plate!

It was as a pitcher that he was signed by the New York Yankees. The Yankees kept him two years, then let him get away in the draft to the Houston Astros. At Houston, not nearly mature as a player, he wasted away on the bench, his skills never developing. When the trade with Houston came along he went in as the unknown quantity. Given the chance at Cincinnati he became the best defensive centerfielder in the National League.

A bargain? Yes, but nothing compared to Griffey.

Griffey was selected by the Reds in the twenty-ninth round of the 1969 player draft, so low that the Reds didn't even waste a phone call telling him they had drafted him. Instead, his notice came in the form of a letter. And Ken Griffey remembers that June day when the letter arrived.

"Hey, Mom," he shouted, "I just been drafted."

"Oh, no," cried Mrs. Griffey. "You gotta go in the Army?"

Griffey explained this was a different draft, the baseball draft.

"I didn't know what being drafted on the twenty-ninth round meant until I got my bonus," says Griffey. "A red jacket and four pairs of sanitary socks. It wasn't even a Cincinnati Reds' jacket. It didn't have an emblem on it. It was just red."

When Ken Griffey reported to Tampa, Florida, he was thrown directly into a game. It wasn't long before he was ready to go home. "I played for Bradenton, and Don Gullett and Ross Grimsley pitched for Sioux Falls," recalls Griffey. "Can you imagine? I tried to hit against Gullett and Grimsley. I was sick. I had two chances — slim and none. Make that one chance — none."

Griffey was as raw as cattle on the hoof, displaying only size and speed. And to top it off he really didn't like to run. "The track coach wanted me to run in the relays but I refused," he said, referring to the track coach at Donora, Pennsylvania High which, incidentally, is the same school that produced Stan Musial. "I stuck to the high jump and broad jump."

Griffey did have one situation in which he liked to run. It was playing football. He was a split end, a pretty good one if you can judge by the statistics. But listen to him talk about his football experiences and you have to wonder.

"I liked to run when I caught a pass and the defender was behind me chasing me. I wasn't about to let him catch up. I didn't like to be hit. There was too much commotion in football. I hated it when I had to make a crack-back block on the defensive end—mainly because he always looked 6-foot-9 and 290 pounds.

"I'd throw a block at his shoes and the guy would kick me away and say, 'Go away, little man.' I only weighed 160 pounds."

Ken Griffey, when he finally became a major league star, was known for his speed. He collected thirty-eight infield hits in 1975. But he says he wasn't always all that fast. "I couldn't think I was that fast, not when my younger brother, Freddie, could outrun me," he smiles. "Fact is all four of my brothers were faster than me. The only one in my family I could outrun was my sister, Ruby, and when she wanted something she could catch me."

Griffey's baseball experience was, like Geronimo's, amazingly limited since his high school team played only sixteen games in four years! "Seems like it rains there every day. The most games we got in during one season was six and we had to play a doubleheader to do that."

American Legion ball was out, too. Griffey didn't make the team. "The coach's son played centerfield," explained Griffey.

Geronimo and Griffey came cheap and became stand-outs quickly and unexpectedly.

That brings us to the discovery of George Foster and the way he was stolen away from the San Francisco Giants. In the winter between the pennant winning year of 1970 and the disaster of 1971, centerfielder Bobby Tolan ruptured his Achilles tendon and was to be out all season.

The Reds tried everything to fill the gap in center. They tried Hal McRae there and while he did an adequate job the club wasn't winning. They tried Pete Rose there. They went out and got Buddy Bradford and gave him the job. He didn't work out. As the season progressed the need remained for an outfielder. Meanwhile, Bob Howsam had another problem on his hands. He was blessed with three young, talented shortstops in Dave Concepcion, Darrel Chaney, and Frank Duffy, a graduate of Stanford University and a college All-American. Of the three, it was decided that Concepcion and Chaney would stay with the big league club, Duffy being shipped to the minor leagues. No thank you, said Duffy, I'm quitting baseball.

"We liked all three of them," recalls Howsam. "We just felt that while Duffy was a good hitter, he didn't have the arm to fill in as a utility player and that's what we needed." Duffy went to Howsam and asked him to try and place him elsewhere. Reluctantly, Howsam agreed to see if he could work out some kind of deal with another organization that would keep Duffy in the major leagues. Two organizations were interested—San Francisco and Pittsburgh. Each had an outfielder or two the Reds were interested in.

Rex Bowen, one of Howsam's superspies, was sent to Charleston, West Virginia to look in on the Pirates' prospect. Howsam, meanwhile, picked up the telephone and called his other super-scout Ray Shore, who was scouting on the West Coast at the time.

"I'm flying to Phoenix," said Howsam. "Meet me at the airport there. We're going to look at a ball player."

Howsam caught the next plane to Phoenix, was greeted by Shore and they drove to the stadium. The Giants had two outfielders that were available for Duffy. One was Bernie Williams, the other, Foster.

"We actually had better reports from our scout in the area on Williams, although the report on Foster wasn't bad," recalls Howsam. Howsam and Shore watched the first seven innings of the game. Foster didn't really do anything to distinguish himself.

"But we could tell he could run and he could throw. He looked like he could hit and he was built like he might have some power although we didn't see it that day," he says.

In the seventh inning Howsam left his seat, went to the back of the stadium where a pay phone was located, and called his office in Cincinnati, looking for Rex Bowen to get his report. Bowen had not yet returned. "Well, find him and have him call me here. I'm at a pay phone and I'll be waiting for his call," instructed Howsam. He was ready to move and move fast.

Twenty minutes went by before the pay phone rang. Howsam lifted the receiver and got Bowen's report. "We're going for one of the two men here," he said. He went back to his seat just as the game was about to end. He told Ray Shore what he was going to do and Shore agreed with him. Off to the Giants' offices he went to speak to Rosie Ryan, the man who was just about running the team at the time.

For a couple of hours they spoke and finally agreed that George Foster would come to the Cincinnati Reds in exchange for Duffy and an overweight pitcher named Vern Geishert.

Geishert retired before ever throwing a pitch for the

Giants. Duffy went to the Giants but never did serve them too well, the Giants using him along with a pitcher named Gaylord Perry to lure Sam McDowell from Cleveland, a trade they have long regretted. Perry became a Cy Young Award winner, and Duffy the regular shortstop at Cleveland. McDowell wound up with his release from San Francisco, the bottle having robbed him of the quickness that once labeled him "Sudden Sam McDowell."

George Foster was not happy to leave the Giants. He was a shy, quiet, almost timid type. He idolized Willie Mays. He had grown up in California. But in baseball you play with whoever owns your contract and now Foster's contract was owned by The Big Red Machine. So he came to Cincinnati, was shoved into the lineup and did a decent job, though hitting only .241.

The next season was a disaster for Foster who hit .200 and played sparsely as Tolan returned. But there was one moment of glory, Foster scoring the run that won the fifth and final playoff game from Pittsburgh on a wild pitch by Bob Moose.

The following season he was at Indianapolis for most of the year. It was to be the turning point of his career. Unknown to the Reds, George Foster twice had been hit in the head with baseballs. He had a deep-seated, unknown fear of the ball. Because of it he had trouble handling the breaking pitches.

"I was reading an article about Maury Wills," Foster now recalls. "This was back when Wills was still playing. He hurt his leg and was afraid to steal bases because he feared he'd mess it up worse. He went to a hypnotist and he helped him get over his fear."

Foster was impressed. He got on the phone to Brooks Lawrence, a former Cincinnati pitcher now in the Cincinnati front office, and the man who has become father confessor to the Reds' black players. He asked what Brooks thought about him going to a hypnotist.

"Go ahead," said Lawrence.

So George Foster took money out of his own pocket and went to see the hypnotist. He was put under for fifteen minutes each time he went over a two-month period. It was the best investment George Foster ever made. A deeply religious man, Foster looks upon the visit to the hypnotist as the turning point in his career.

"It was," he says, "a religious experience. God works through other people. If you need His help, He'll give it to you. By believing in the hypnotist I was believing in God."

George Foster went the long route to stardom as did Geronimo and Griffey. But get there they did, forming an outfield that was as good as any in the big leagues. They were overshadowed, true, by that million-dollar infield. But they gained respect.

"They don't get the recognition they should get 'cause they're so young," says Anderson. "But just wait two years. They won't be overshadowed then."

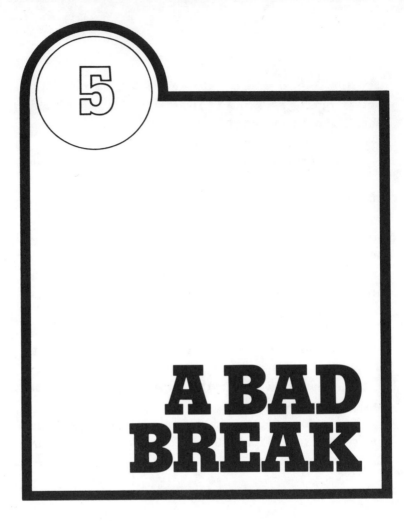

5

A BAD BREAK

By the 16th of June the city of Cincinnati knew that it had something special in 1975, something more than just another baseball team. They were anticipating a summer season to end all other summer seasons. The race, they figured, would be tight, the Reds and the Dodgers all the way to the wire. Already they were buying tickets for the Dodger series in September, still a couple of months in the future.

Pete Rose had moved from his left field "Rose

Garden" to third base and the fans in the left-field seats had become "Foster's Fanatics," the residents of "Fosterville."

The hard times had come and gone, and as the song that every Cincinnatian knows, goes:

"The whole town is batty about Cincinnati, what a team, what a team, what a team. Each man and lady, from eight to eighty, how they scream, how they scream, how they scream."

Fountain Square, a beautiful square in the heart of downtown, was abuzz every day with the doings of the Reds. It seemed like they never lost. Everyone was playing as if this were *The Year.*

The Reds had spurted into a three and a half game lead over the Dodgers and it figured to be no less, maybe more if the Dodgers would cooperate and lose on the night of June 16.

After all, Don Gullett was pitching for the Reds and everyone knew that a team like the Atlanta Braves wasn't going to beat Don Gullett. He was coming off a complete game victory over the St. Louis Cardinals. In the two and a half months already expired in the season he had lost just three games.

"Don Gullett, if he doesn't get hurt, will be in the Hall of Fame when his career is over," crowed manager Sparky Anderson. He was that kind of pitcher. He was that kind of athlete.

Don Gullett had been brought up in Reds' country, having spent his life on a farm in Lynn, Kentucky, a little town across the Ohio River from Portsmouth, Ohio. He was something of a legend in the area. In one high school football game, playing for McKell High (Lynn being far too small to have a school of its own), he scored seventy-two points. That figured out to eleven touchdowns and six extra points. Don Gullett had a reputation as the best running back in the area. Locals said maybe even the best running back anywhere.

As Gullett now recalls it he was undecided about playing football his senior year. He had been bothered by ankles that seemed to sprain without provocation and he knew that the baseball scouts were interested in him.

At the last possible moment, with some urging from friends, Don Gullett decided that he would play football. He went out for the team late and was anything but ready when McKell went against Wurtland High in a scrimmage. He was used for only three plays on offense, doing very little. "Oh," he remembers modestly, "I did intercept a pass and go for a touchdown."

The next day the local papers, though, were full of quotes from the opposition about how they had handled Gullett. This didn't set too well with the McKell coach. Neither did the quotes that came out before the two schools were to meet in the regular season game. "We're gonna stop Gullett. We're gonna put him out of the game," said the men from Wurtland. "This kinda made coach mad. He decided to turn me loose," Gullett explained.

The final score was McKell 72, Wurtland 6. All seventy-two points belonged to Gullett. "And," says Gullett, "a couple of other guys scored touchdowns, but they were called back." Eleven touchdowns in a high school football game. Of such stuff are legends born.

The legend continued to grow as Don Gullett led the state of Kentucky in scoring. Autumn passed into winter and Gullett changed sports. He played basketball averaging better than twenty points a game.

But it was neither football nor basketball that could collar Don Gullett. Baseball was his game. With his brother,

Bill, teaching him just about everything he knew, he became the most talked about young pitcher in the midwest. In one game where a Cincinnati scout happened to be present Gullett struck out twenty of the twenty-one hitters he faced in a seven-inning no-hitter. It came as no suprise that in 1969 the Reds made him their Number 1 draft choice.

Turning down college scholarship offers to play football, he signed with the Reds. When the Reds signed Don Gullett they knew they had something special on their hands. He went to Sioux Falls in 1969 and was 7-2 with a 1.95 earned run average, lowest in the league.

In 1970, being all of eighteen years old, he made the Reds. It was reminiscent of Gary Nolan a few years earlier, who came out of Class A ball to make the team and go on to win fourteen games.

Gullett was used out of the bull pen, winning five, losing two, stringing together a 2.42 earned run average. He pitched four innings in the playoffs that year, not allowing a run, and was a bit of a sensation in the World Series, pitching seven innings and giving up just one run.

Hard luck had followed Gullett's career, though. After a 16-6 season in 1971 he suffered from hepatitis, dropping to 9-10 in 1972. In 1973, still weak from the hepatitis, Gullett was amazing, winning eighteen and losing eight. He followed that up in 1974 with a 17-11 record. By the time the 1975 season rolled around, he was considered the "stopper," a baseball term for a pitcher who keeps a team from going into a long losing streak by winning whenever it is really needed.

Gullett owned the best winning percentage in baseball of pitchers with a hundred decisions or more at .637. Already, at twenty-four he had won sixty-five big league games. By age twenty-four the great Warren Spahn had not yet won a game and Sandy Koufax had won but twenty. Gullett was on his way to greatness.

His start on June 16 was a sight to behold. After eight innings Atlanta could show only four hits, one of them a home run by Cito Gaston. The Reds, meanwhile, had gone to work on the Braves. In the bottom of the eighth, leading 3-1, they exploded for six runs.

During the game Gullett had shown what kind of player he was, not only by pitching with perfection but by hitting a triple and a sacrifice fly.

The ninth inning was to be just a formality, the Reds on top 9-1 and Gullett in complete command. But Gullett was running out of gas in a hurry. He gave up a single. He got an out. Then two more singles. It was 9-2 and Larvell Blanks, the Atlanta shortstop they call "Sugar Bear," was at the plate. Gullett threw and Blanks sent a line drive screaming back at the mound. There was panic. Gullett had been hit. He had been hit in the pitching hand.

The ball went to second base where Blanks was thrown out. But no one seemed to notice. All eyes were on Gullett as he writhed in pain. He gazed at the hand. Swelling had begun. Clearly, as if burned into the skin, the outline of the stitches on the baseball could be seen.

"I think it's broken," said Gullett.

Larry Starr, the team trainer, took a look at it. He asked Gullett to move the fingers. They didn't move. He immediately froze the injury. It was starting to hemorrhage. It was swelling and turning blue.

Don Gullett was carted off to Christ Hospital for X-rays. They weren't really necessary. Anderson and Starr talked about Gullett when he was gone, said they were hoping for the best, said they didn't think there was a break. Then came the word. Don Gullett had suffered a broken thumb. Worse yet, the impact had carried the break down into the wrist joint.

When next seen, Don Gullett had a cast on his wrist. He was to be out of action for at least six weeks in the heart of a pennant race, a race where an injury could be the difference between winning and losing. The Number 1 starter on the Cincinnati Reds' pitching staff — a staff that was maligned and called inadequate — was out.

It was a dark day. Tom Carroll was recalled from Indianapolis to try and fill some of the void. "You never really replace a Don Gullett," said Anderson. The next night the Reds lost and the lead was two and a half games. The whole town was getting edgy about the Reds. At The Cricket, a local bar in the heart of the downtown area, they talked about the Reds and they were not talking about winning a pennant. Instead, they were saying the end had begun. The populace figured that in no way could the Reds hang on.

So what happened? The Reds won three in a row, lost a game, then won six in a row. They had won nine of eleven since the injury.

Don Gullett did not pitch again until August 18. But instead of collapsing, The Big Red Machine had come to life. When Gullett returned — ironically on the same night that it was learned that shortstop Dave Concepcion had a broken bone in his right wrist — the Reds were in front by seventeen and a half games. With Gullett out they had won forty-four and lost fourteen. The lead had swelled from three and a half games to seventeen and a half.

The race was over by then. But how? How could the Reds have done it without their Number 1 pitcher?

They did it because "Captain Hook" maneuvered his pitchers as pitchers had never before been maneuvered. He had come up with the bull pen of bull pens, the ultimate in a relief corps.

He had not one outstanding relief pitcher, as some teams have, nor two, nor three. He had *four* outstanding relief pitchers, two of them proven veterans, two untried kids.

The Reds set a major league record by going forty-five games in a row without a complete game, a record that could lead one to believe that the starters had failed so completely that disaster must have come. Of the forty-five games they won thirty-two.

They had done it with the bull pen. Complete games?

"I just wish," said pitching coach Larry Shepard, who complimented and chastised, punished and rewarded, psyched and created this staff, "they would do away with the complete game statistic. What does it mean? All that matters is if you won or if you lost. We don't look at a game as being something for a pitcher to win or lose. We look at each game as being a challenge for the entire staff."

Indeed, the Reds used a concept that no one before them had dared to use. Day after day Anderson would call on this pitcher, then that pitcher. He did it as need arose. Personal records, personal goals were given a back seat.

On June 30, for example, his starter Tom Carroll didn't make it out of the second inning, the Reds trailing 4-0. By the time the third inning started he had his third pitcher in the game. That was Pedro Borbon. He pitched six innings and gave up eleven hits. Still the game went on. Will McEnaney came on in the ninth and Clay Kirby in the tenth. Kirby pitched the final three innings. The Reds won in the bottom of the twelfth on a three-run homer by Johnny Bench.

The bull pen, though, had won the game. Not Bench.

Not any one pitcher. All four relievers who had been used.

The next night the Reds played fifteen innings against Houston, it taking four hours and twenty-one minutes to complete the game. Anderson used six pitchers. He won the game.

Anderson showed no hint of hesitation in going to the bull pen. He went no matter what the situation. He went whenever he got the urge. And they booed him in Cincinnati.

What did it matter? He walked to the mound with his head down, seemingly listing to the right side, careful to skip over the foul line as was his superstition. He got to the mound, held out a hand and said, "Not tonight." No one argued with him. They left. They understood. They knew the results.

The bull pen had become as much a part of The Big Red Machine as Joe Morgan, Johnny Bench, Pete Rose, and Tony Perez. Maybe even a bigger part.

Who are these men? Clay Carroll. Pedro Borbon. Will McEnaney. Rawlins Jackson Eastwick III, who was called "Rawly." In many ways, they differed greatly but they all had one thing in common. They were flakes, a flake being a baseball term for someone who views life and lives in a way that is somewhat out of the ordinary — by baseball standards anyway.

McEnaney readily admits it. "Hey," he says, "I pride myself on being flaky." He recalls the first time George Zuraw, a Cincinnati scout, saw him.

"You're just flaky enough to make it to the major leagues," Zuraw told McEnaney.

Being flaky and being a relief pitcher go hand-in-hand. Ask Joe Page or Jim Brosnan, or Al Hrabowsky. The normal personality does not lend itself to the life. Time after time the relief pitcher is asked to enter a contest with the outcome on the line, with the win about to belong to someone else. He is often asked to get out the other side's best hitter.

If he succeeds, well, that's what he was supposed to do. "Nice going," say the guys. But if he fails, if he comes in and gives up a home run, he takes a loss, no one speaks to him and the fans chastise him and the manager.

"How could they bring that bum in?" they'll ask, knowing full well if the ball somehow had been caught they would have called it a fine relief job. The relief pitcher takes the most pressure there is in baseball. Sometimes it can get to him. It once got to McEnaney.

He was at Indianapolis, the Reds' top farm club, and the job he did on this particular night in Wichita was something less than spectacular. He retired to the locker room where he promptly dismantled a couple of wooden tools, leaving nothing more than a million toothpicks. He tore two screens off dressing cages. In his rage he took off his spikes and sent them flying against the wall.

Vern Rapp was managing Indianapolis and, like his young pitcher, he was known to throw a tantrum or two. Still, he figured he had to teach McEnaney a lesson. He told him there were other left-handers who would like the opportunity to make it to the American Association.

"I got the message," recalls McEnaney.

After that, McEnaney had to pay a security deposit every time he visited Wichita, a bit of negative psychology that never did work for Wichita, the thinking being that McEnaney again would be hit hard and throw a tantrum. Neither happened.

"I decided to curb my temper for fear of hurting my

wallet and my physical well-being," he recalls.

Will McEnaney is a flake. Take his act on the team bus after a loss. For some reason still not fully explained, a professional baseball team following a loss is supposed to act as if a close relative had become a member of the dearly departed. No talking, no smiling.

Not McEnaney. He'll sit in the back of the bus and chatter away, smiling, laughing. A man will walk past the bus and he'll hear this anonymous voice shout, "Sir, you dropped your wallet." The passerby will stop dead in his tracks, wheel around on his heels and search for the imaginary wallet as McEnaney laughs away.

"Childish but fun," says McEnaney. "I just can't sit there after a loss. I mean, so what if we lost a couple of games. It's not that important, is it? So I smile."

Will McEnaney has always been something offbeat, out of the ordinary. He grew up as did Gullett in Reds' country in Springfield, Ohio. He married his hometown sweetheart in a love affair that got off to a typically McEnaney start.

Having seen Daryl Lynne for the first time, he was attracted but needed some way to start a conversation. McEnaney approached the lady:

"Hi, my name is Will McEnaney. How do you like me so far?"

"I don't," she answered.

Soon, she did. As did everyone around Springfield except for his high school baseball coach. Seems McEnaney liked beer in high school almost as much as he liked baseball. He wound up only with the beer, having been told to sever his relations with the baseball team.

A talent like McEnaney's doesn't go unnoticed and the

Reds wound up drafting him, schooling him through the minor leagues and making him into the left-handed star of a bull pen that was star-studded.

McEnaney was one half of Captain Hook's "Kiddie Korps." The other half was a tall, cocky, skinny right-hander. His name sounded as if he should be sitting on the veranda of a pre-Civil War plantation sipping a mint julep and courting Linda Sue, the belle of the country.

Rawlins Jackson Eastwick III isn't exactly the kind of name you find on a street fighter but that is just the kind of relief pitcher Eastwick is. He comes at you like it's a personal battle and he lets you know right away that he's the boss.

"My name helped me get to the big leagues. It made me noticed. But it's my arm that keeps me there," he says. "I like the challenge. That's what I'm here for."

The 1975 season for Rawly Eastwick started on a sour note. He was assigned to the minor leagues and didn't like it. But he could do nothing about it, nothing other than go down and pitch impressively until he was needed. And he was needed sooner than he thought.

"It really hurt when I went to the minor leagues but I made up my mind that I'd think nothing but positive thoughts. I knew I'd be back," he recalls. When the Reds gave up on John Vukovich at third base, they recalled Eastwick. It was May 15. He had missed five weeks of the season. "The bull pen needed a shot in the arm. I think I did it," he says, not the least bit modestly.

Not that he was any ball of fire when he was recalled. Anderson, taking him on right away as his pet threw him in as the Number 1 relief pitcher and it was almost disaster. He wasn't getting anyone out.

One day in June, pitching coach Larry Shepard called

Eastwick into his office. "Kid," said Shepard, "just who do you think is going to the minor leagues when Don Gullett's hand mends?"

No answer was necessary. Eastwick knew it was him.

"You're pressing. You're trying to make your pitches too fine. Just go out there and throw the ball. Throw it as hard as you can. You can do it," lectured Shepard. He had made his point. Rawly Eastwick did not want to return to the minor leagues. He knew he was a better pitcher than he had shown. He was now inspired.

The next day Anderson asked him to perform a miracle, the kind of miracle relief pitchers perform every day. It was a game against the Philadelphia Phillies, bases loaded, two out in the bottom of the eighth, the Reds on top by a run.

Mike Schmidt, the National League's home run king was the batter. Three pitches later the inning was over. "It was a game we had to win," Eastwick remembers. "The Dodgers were right with us at the time. So I struck Schmidt out and we won. That kept everybody's head together."

A couple of days later the Reds were in New York leading 2-1, two on in the ninth inning and with two out. Dave Kingman, a dead fast ball hitter and perhaps the most powerful man in the game, was batting. Eastwick challenged him, threw him three fast balls, all strikes.

"I stair-stepped him," said Eastwick. "A low fast ball, a higher fast ball and then a high fast ball. With two strikes no one can lay off my high fast ball." No one seemed to be able to hit it, either. Eastwick was that kind of relief pitcher. It all goes back, he says, to positive thinking.

"Positive thoughts radiate," he says. "Maybe people can tell you're having positive thoughts."

People, to Eastwick in this case, are hitters.

"If you look like you're going to get him out—if you look like you're going to throw strikes—if you look like you're going to keep the ball down—if you look like you're going to get him out you will."

If you get the idea that Rawlins Jackson Eastwick III fits right in with McEnaney as a bit of a flake, if for no other reason than his confidence, you're right. He is a bit strange. This is especially true when it comes to his arm.

The modern day baseball player is always being looked upon by the player of the past as something of a pussycat. "We used to spit in spike wounds," the former player will say. "Rub dirt in it, that's all. We'd laugh at injuries."

Sometimes the man has a point. Prior to game time 1975, the busiest place in a baseball park is the trainer's room, players fighting for space in the whirlpool, undergoing ultrasound treament, having an ankle taped or an arm rubbed.

Rawly Eastwick isn't sure where the trainer's room is.

"My philosophy," he explains, "is the best thing for your arm is nothing. Nobody can touch my arm and I mean nobody. I don't do nothing to it. No arm rub. No hot stuff. I don't believe in milking your arm and all that and I don't believe in rubbing it down."

To a pitcher his arm is his only asset. When that goes he's through. The two veterans who made up The Big Red Machine's bull pen, Clay Carroll and Pedro Borbon, know this. Both were born with exceptional throwing arms. Both fit in as kooks and men who are unbothered by pressure.

It is Carroll, perhaps, who best symbolizes what the relief pitcher is. Clay Carroll grew up in Clanton, Alabama, a little town a couple of hours southwest of Atlanta. He has memories of the cotton mill there, working and slaving for long hours and short pay. His father did it for forty years.

102

He did it himself, taking on the dirtiest of jobs. And he didn't like it.

"Without this arm of mine, I'd still be a-workin' in that thar mill," he drawls.

Cotton Mill Hill they called it. In Clanton there were 5,000 people and five traffic lights. That was town. That was the world to Clay Carroll, one of eight children, six brothers and a sister.

None of the Carrolls knew much about baseball except for Clay who kept sneaking away to play the game. Not that he had a whole lot of time to play the game of baseball. There were chores around the house and on weekends it was those long, miserable hours working in the cotton mill, cleaning the frames that compressed the bales of cotton. They were oily, greasy, and messy.

"Someday," he vowed, "I'm a-gettin' outa here."

That someday came in 1961. By this time Clay Carroll had worked in the mill, worked as a carhop at a drive-in restaurant, loaded watermelons on a truck, something he's forever grateful for as it developed the strength of the then rail-thin kid.

Dixie Walker, a scout for the Milwaukee Braves, drove into Clanton one afternoon in '61. He was toting some money, more than Clay Carroll knew existed in the world. A whole thousand dollars.

"That was ninety-nine thousand less than they were givin' to a lot of guys in those days; to me it was one-hundred thousand," Carroll recalls. His parents were mystified. They didn't know much about this game their son was going to play, but they knew what $1,000 was and they saw a chance for him to make some money.

Clay Carroll signed. He took the check, marveled at it, then went to the bank and deposited it in a checking account. It stayed in the account a couple of hours. Clay Carroll immediately went out and bought himself a used car for $750.

"I got me a fifty-four Ford," he recalls. "A real classic then."

Clay Carroll was tired of walking. "I didn't have me no bike," he says. "These was my bike." He pointed at his feet.

Clay Carroll decided to show off his bright, shiny, powerful new car to his cousins. He piled 'em in and drove off on one of those nearly deserted gravel roads that dissect Alabama.

"I was a-showin' off," says Carroll. "I went out and put that baby in a spin." That was all it took. Carroll spun that baby right around a tree. End of car.

"I ain't been back down that road since," he says.

Clay Carroll was lucky. He hadn't spent all his bonus money on that '54 Ford. He had enough left to take the train to Waycross, Georgia and his first spring training.

It was, he remembers, not exactly the most pleasant of experiences. They were housed in an old Army base.

"If you wasn't in by midnight you didn't get in," he says. "They locked the gates."

No car, not much money, a country boy lost in the outside world. All Clay Carroll had was his arm and he put it to use.

He became one of the premier relief pitchers in baseball, earning in the exclusive neighborhood of $95,000 a year.

"Not bad," he says.

Clanton is nothing but a memory, although he returns home every winter as a celebrity, the only celebrity the town has ever had. One winter they even held a Clay Carroll Day and retired his high school football jersey.

"Quite an honor, eh?" he asks, quite seriously.

Cincinnati Reds' relief pitcher Will McEnaney is known as a flake. Here, before a game, he sits on the dugout railing and stares pensively at the crowd. In another move, he blows a bubble in the Reds' locker room, taking part in a contest that he lost to Johnny Bench.
—Terry Armor, Cincinnati Post Photos

A familiar sight, catcher Johnny Bench congratulating young right-handed relief pitcher Rawly Eastwick after a save. Eastwick, in his first big league season, tied for the National League lead in saves with 22.
—*Terry Armor, Cincinnati Post Photo*

The ace of the Cincinnati pitching staff, Don Gullett, points a finger as he begins delivery to Atlanta's Ralph Garr.
—*Fred Straub, Cincinnati Enquirer Photo*

Trainer Larry Starr leads Don Gullett to the locker room after Larvell Blanks' line drive struck the ace of the Cincinnati pitching staff on the left hand, breaking his thumb.
—*Wide World Photos*

Ted Sizemore is too late with his tag as the Reds' Ken Griffey steals second base against St. Louis.—*Fred Straub, Cincinnati Enquirer Photo*

The Reds, including Jack Billingham, right, and Ted Kluszewski give George Foster congratulations after a home run. —*Terry Armor, Cincinnati Post Photo*

Young Jack Billingham gives his best "fast ball" to Pete Rose as his father, Jack the pitcher, catches during a break in the spring training routine. —*Fred Straub, Cincinnati Enquirer Photo*

Gary Nolan, who overcame two years of arm troubles and surgery, works for the Reds in one of his 15 victories that helped to the runaway Western Division championship.
—*Terry Armor, Cincinnati Post Photo*

Given a chance to play,
George Foster provided
The Big Red Machine
with both speed and
power. Here he steals
second against Boston in
the World Series as
Denny Doyle covers.
Then he is congratulated
at the plate by Tony
Perez after a home run.
—*Terry Armor, Cincinnati
Post Photos*

Johnny Bench, owner of more Gold Gloves for defensive excellence than any catcher in baseball history, performs some magic as he grabs foul pop in front of the screen with one hand.—*Terry Armor, Cincinnati Post Photo*

Sparky Anderson (l) and former Reds' great Ted Kluszewski become totally involved during a tense moment in the National League playoffs.
—*Fred Straub, Cincinnati Enquirer Photo*

Today he lives in Bradenton, Florida. "Got me a house with a swimming pool," he says. "Really something." Clay Carroll, because of his country upbringing and because he is not possessed of the quickest mind in the world, takes a bit of a ripping from his teammates.

But Carroll says, "I can take a rip."

He has to. After the 1970 World Series he went to Johnny Bench and Pete Rose and bought a Continental Mark IV from their car dealership. That's about as far removed from a '54 Ford as Riverfront Stadium is from Cotton Mill Hill. He arrived the next spring in Tampa with the new car. And what kind of reception did he get?

"Clay Carroll with a Mark Four is like putting earrings on a hog," laughed Tommy Helms, then the Reds' second baseman.

Yes, Carroll could take a rip and most of them came from Helms.

In 1970 the Reds moved into Riverfront Stadium and Helms hit the first Cincinnati home run in the new park. Not exactly a majestic shot, the ball barely cleared the fence and struck against the foul screen.

Early the next day Carroll and his roommate, Wayne Granger, decided that the historic spot should be marked. They sneaked out early and on the spot hit by the home run placed a large X made from adhesive tape.

Helms came out, took one look at the work and said: "That had to be Carroll. He left his signature."

There is in Clay Carroll a lot of Dizzy Dean. As it was with ol' Diz, the only thing that matters to Carroll is baseball. He didn't worry much about schoolwork. In fact when he was signed at age nineteen, he was so eager to "git goin'," as he put it, that he decided to forego the final three months of his education.

"I wanted to git to spring training," he explains.

Not that he didn't get his degree. "About three years later the principal gave it to me. Sort of an honorary degree I guess," he now says.

Carroll can see the resemblance between himself and Dizzy Dean.

"Guess I'm like ol' Diz was," he admits. "I mean from the way he talked on television—when he wasn't singing 'The Wabash Cannonball'—he just reared back and threw that fast ball.

"That's what I do. Diz didn't sound like he pitched to spots and I don't either. I jest bring it."

To the Reds Clay Carroll is "The Hawk," a nickname bestowed upon him in honor of a nose that looks like a beak. When he's asleep the sounds that come out of that nose sound not like any creature living or dead. He rooms alone because of his snoring. Jim Maloney, once a Reds' pitcher, tried to room with him one year. It lasted about a week.

"I woke up one morning," Carroll recalls, "and Maloney had a cover and a pillow in the closet. He was sound asleep in there."

"I could still hear him snoring even with the door shut," says Maloney.

What Clay Carroll can do is pitch. During the 1975 season he broke Joe Nuxhall's all-time record for most appearances by a Cincinnati Reds' pitcher. Still, with the emergence of McEnaney and Eastwick he was relegated to a secondary role.

"It kinda hurts me," he admitted one night. "I can still pitch. I'm gonna pitch til I'm forty, maybe longer. The good Lord gave me this arm and I've got to use it."

Pedro Borbon is in many ways like Carroll. He was blessed with an arm that is tireless. However, like many Latin Americans—Borbon being a native of the Dominican

Republic—he has a temper that puts him in the midst of great predicaments.

Perhaps the two most memorable moments in the career of Pedro Borbon occurred during free-for-alls on the field. The first came in the midst of "The Battle of Shea Stadium." It was the third game of the 1973 playoffs, the Reds facing the New York Mets.

With the Mets leading, a fight broke out as Pete Rose slid hard into Bud Harrelson, the little New York shortstop, attempting to break up a double play. Both benches emptied immediately.

In the Cincinnati bull pen Borbon saw the two teams fighting. He rushed to the gate of the bull pen, tried to get it open but the gate seemed to be jammed shut. So, intent on getting out, Borbon ripped the gate right off its hinges as he and his bull pen playmates rushed into the action.

By the time Borbon arrived things seemed to be calming down with Ted Kluszewski and Johnny Bench muscling Rose out of the melee and players just milling around. A typical baseball fight. It seemed Borbon had missed the action. That wouldn't do. He needed to fight now so he hauled off on Buzz Capra, a little-used New York relief pitcher. It was every man for himself again, Borbon having instigated an entirely new battle.

Fifteen minutes later some semblance of peace was restored. But there was no peace within the flaming personality of Borbon. He started toward the Cincinnati dugout reaching down for his baseball cap.

In his anger, though, Borbon got not his cap but the cap belonging to Cleon Jones of the Mets. He put it on his head, then suddenly reached up and grabbed the cap. "I put on the cap and all I see is blue, not red like my cap," Borbon recalls.

He took the cap in his mouth and took a tremendous bite out of it as he walked toward the dugout. Then he began ripping away piece by piece, bringing about one of the most comical sights ever seen on a baseball field.

Here was Borbon tearing away at the baseball cap, taking each little piece and flinging it as he walked toward the dugout. And right behind him gathering up each piece as he threw it, was Cleon Jones trying to save his shredded cap.

Borbon's second moment of glory occurred during the 1974 season. The Reds had just won four straight from Pittsburgh in a five-game series when a fight broke out after Bruce Kison and Jack Billingham became involved in a beanball battle.

Borbon, as could be expected, found himself right in the middle of the action. He wound up paired off with Daryl Patterson, a Pittsburgh relief pitcher. The two wrestled on the ground, Borbon finally gaining the advantage as he tugged away at Patterson's hair, removing whole tufts of it.

But the moment of truth came when Borbon sank his teeth deeply into Patterson's side. When it all was over and cooler heads prevailed Daryl Patterson found himself at a Pittsburgh hospital for a tetanus shot.

Borbon found some small measure of fame in the episode as Bob Prince, the Pirates' long-time radio voice, began calling Borbon "Dracula." The nickname did not sit well with Borbon. When the Reds arrived in Pittsburgh for their first meeting of 1975 Borbon decided it was time to put an end to his new nickname.

Rain was falling as players stood in the dugout. Nellie King, a former major league pitcher who was the color commentator with Prince, was there as Borbon approached.

"You know my name?" said Borbon.

"Yes, Pedro Borbon," answered King.

"Borbon, not Dracula," said Borbon.

"I never called you anything but Pedro Borbon," said King.

Borbon suddenly realized that he had the wrong man. "You tell the other guy I no like the name Dracula," instructed Borbon.

"I don't carry messages. Tell him yourself," said King.

Now Borbon was mad. "Maybe you want me to punch you in the nose," said Borbon. King just walked away. "He was serious," King later related.

Of such things, though, are relief pitchers made and when you have four of them, as did The Big Red Machine, you had it all. Anderson knew this. Asked one day where he'd be without his bull pen, he merely replied: "Back home in Thousand Oaks, California."

6

THE RETURN OF GARY NOLAN

Spring training for a major league baseball player is anything but Sparta revisited. The idea, it says somewhere, is to drive the players into shape, make them sweat off the fat accumulated over a winter on the banquet circuit, tone the muscles for the long, grueling season that lies ahead.

Yes sir, sure is tough work. Six weeks in the Florida sunshine when back north the weatherman is saying:

"The high today will be eighteen. There's a fifty

percent chance that it will snow with an accumulation of about three inches expected. Don't forget your snow tires." And the ballplayer laughs, grabs his golf bag and heads out to the course.

Oh, there is work for the players, a long, hard day on the field. Compared to most camps the one run by Sparky Anderson for the Cincinnati Reds is a concentration camp. The workouts are long, the emphasis on fundamentals, with so much running that a player soon wonders whether he's training to play shortstop or run in the Boston Marathon.

The days starts early — for a baseball player — dressed and on the field at ten a.m. There is a half hour of calisthenics, then wind sprints, then fundamental drills. That is followed by batting practice, long batting practice with Pete Rose, Tony Perez, Joe Morgan, Dave Concepcion, and Johnny Bench never tiring. They hit until blisters form on their hands, softened by a winter of inactivity. Then the blisters break and the blood begins to trickle out and they go on hitting, forming calluses where the blisters once were.

The pitchers follow a different routine. As the batters hit they stand around the outfield and shag fly balls until it is their turn to pitch batting practice.

The muscles become stiff and sore for a couple of days but when the workout is over at two p.m. or so, the day belongs to the player. For most of the Cincinnati Reds this means a return to the apartment or hotel, the apartment having been subleased for the spring. The children are in Florida, most of them receiving lessons from a tutor.

Lunch. Maybe golf or tennis or an afternoon fishing. An outdoor barbecue, ribs or chicken, but most likely steak, as the balmy Florida breezes blow. And back home they're shoveling their walks and putting out the sand on the ice.

It's work but the working conditions sure are nice.

For most of the Cincinnati Reds on this spring day in 1974 it was just some more grunting and groaning, get those muscles into shape, toughen the hands, build up the strength. Just push the body to its limit to reach the desired result. The rookies were scurrying everywhere trying to impress Sparky Anderson, trying to make a team that had very few openings.

The veterans were taking it at a more leisurely pace. They had been there before. They knew what had to be done. They were aiming for opening day. It was then that they had to be ready. They were secure in their jobs.

Batting practice was just about over, almost time to suck it in a little bit more and go through the day's second set of sprints. The last pitcher who was to work out that day was on the mound, one of the young kids trying to impress. He was throwing the ball hard and the hitters, not yet sharp, were mumbling to themselves as they fouled one off, swung and missed or ducked away from a high, inside fast ball.

Gary Nolan stood off to one side of the batting cage, sweat running in little rivers off his forehead. He had worked harder than anyone in camp. He took extra exercises. He ran harder, longer, and more often.

His stomach was flat. His muscles bulged. There was only one trouble. Gary Nolan was a pitcher who could not throw a baseball. He turned to Pete Rose. "You know," he said, "I've been dead a year and a half and they haven't given me a funeral."

The words came out with feeling. There was bitterness, yes, but more than that there was sadness. Gary Nolan lived to play baseball. He was better at his trade than most men. He earned a lovely living from the game, roughly $60,000. He knew nothing else.

Gary Nolan was still two months short of his twenty-fifth birthday at the time, yet a seasoned veteran in the world of professional baseball. And his arm was dead. As if that weren't bad enough he could get no one connected with the Cincinnati Reds to believe that his arm actually was as bad as it was. Pain, you see, is a singular experience. No one else can experience your pain. You cannot remember your pain when it is gone.

Yes, said the Reds, Gary Nolan has pain. But a pitcher has to learn to live with pain. They would point to Bob Gibson, the great St. Louis Cardinal, who said his arm hurt with every pitch he threw and that he often refused to shake hands with another person because it shot a pain through his arm. But he pitched.

Maybe history was working against Gary Nolan. He had burst out of nowhere onto the big league scene. The Number 1 draft choice of the Reds in June, 1966, he had been given a tremendous bonus to sign.

When his name was on a contract the first thing the Reds did with their prize was to take him on a road trip, show him life in the big leagues. He was thrilled by it all. Also homesick. He was nothing but a high school kid, already married and the father of a child. And what a trip the Reds chose to take him on. They lost ten games in a row.

Upon returning home the Reds assigned Gary Nolan to Sioux Falls. He pitched twelve games that year, completing nine. His record was 7-3 and his earned run average was 1.82. His fast ball was overpowering. In 104 innings he struck out 163. And he had that God-given gift that so few hard-throwing pitchers have—control. In 104 innings that first minor league season he walked only thirty.

The Reds knew they had something special on their hands. Another year of seasoning they reasoned, and he'd be ready for the big show. No way, said Nolan.

"I'm going to make this team," he said when he reported to spring training in 1967. They guffawed at the kid. He wasn't yet nineteen years old. He had twelve games of professional experience behind him. There is no way you jump from a rookie league to the big leagues.

Gary Nolan is not a boastful sort though. They soon paid attention to him. He turned loose his fast ball day after day. Spring training came to a close and Gary Nolan, eighteen, was a Cincinnati Red and what a Red he was! He strung together a 14-8 record with a 2.58 earned run average. He struck out 206 and walked sixty-two. And there was that one game of which he was so proud.

The San Francisco Giants against the Cincinnati Reds. Gary Nolan, so young, so innocent, facing Willie Mays, Willie McCovey, and the others. And he was blowing them away. In one inning, the Giants loaded the bases.

Reaching back, Nolan struck out Mays. He struck out McCovey. He struck out Jim Ray Hart.

In the eighth inning he had a 3-0 lead and fourteen strikeouts, the last being Mays. It was the fourth time he had fanned The Great One in the game and Mays pointed out, "Nobody's ever done that to me before." Two men were on base.

Willie McCovey came on. No strikeout. Instead, a long home run and a tie ball game. With the crowd giving him a standing ovation that would live in his memory forever, Gary Nolan exited from the game, a game the Reds eventually were to lose.

Gary Nolan was a true phenomenon. But dark clouds were forming and Larry Jansen, the pitching coach for the

Giants, was one man who saw them. "With his motion he's sure to hurt his arm," said Jansen. A year later he was proven correct, Nolan suffering his first arm misery.

Sore arms and the Cincinnati Reds go hand and hand. Over the years, for some inexplicable reason Cincinnati pitchers become one-armed bandits, stealing their salary for not pitching. Jim Maloney, Mel Queen, Billy McCool, Roger Nelson, Jim O'Toole.

The throbbing started in the spring of '68. On April 1, as he was trying to get ready for the opening of the season, Gary Nolan walked off the mound after throwing two pitches in the second inning of an exhibition game.

"We just may," observed Bob Howsam, "send him to the minors to get in shape." The remark shook Nolan. No mention of the pain he was suffering. The indication was, instead, that he was out of shape. He hurt and they figured he was just a kid who didn't know about pain.

A week later, Gary Nolan was in the minor leagues at Tampa. He pitched two games, lasting only five innings. He had a sore arm. The Reds, however, needed that arm, visions of the kid of 1967 still dancing in their head. They called him back to the big leagues. In mid-May, he pitched five innings in an exhibition game. Then, five days later he was booked to throw batting practice. He lasted five minutes, walking off the mound in pain.

"I wouldn't say I'm disgusted," he said. "The word is impatient. Either that or I'm fouled up." It was getting to him. He knew he hurt. No one else could understand it. He wound up having a good season again despite the sore arm, winning nine and losing four with a 2.40 earned run average.

Then came 1969. More of the same. This time it was a freak injury. Trying to spin off a curve ball his spikes caught on the mound. He pulled a muscle in his forearm.

115

Eleven days he sat around, trying to come back against Los Angeles only to be rocked. Two weeks later he was tried in relief against New York, giving up two home runs in one inning.

At this time his record was 1-3 with a 5.29 earned run average. His arm ached and Bob Howsam said:

"After reviewing Gary's performance, both Dave Bristol and I thought it best he be sent to Indianapolis where he'd have the opportunity to work regularly and regain the form he had as a fourteen-game winner in his rookie season, and in the latter portion of 1968 when he was a solid winner."

Again, no mention of injury, no mention of pain, no mention of sore arm. So Gary Nolan went to Indianapolis, pitched thirty-one innings, went 2-0 and was recalled. He came on strong, finishing at 8-8 with a 3.55 earned run average.

The next two years Gary Nolan pitched free of pain, going 18-7 in 1970—a pennant year for the Reds—and 12-15 in 1971, a disastrous year for the Reds.

Gary Nolan now was ready to blossom and blossom he did in 1972. He became the best pitcher in baseball. By this time the fast ball was only a shadow of what it had once been. But he had acquired the most devastating change-up in the big leagues, an elusively slow pitch that would come to the plate and sink and break in any of three directions at once.

"The damn thing comes up there, you see it, you start to swing and it disappears," said Willie Stargell of the Pittsburgh Pirates.

Gary Nolan was on top of the world. He won thirteen of his first fifteen decisions. His earned run average was 1.82. He was a shoo-in for the Cy Young Award. He was named to the National League's All-Star team. Then came the announcement. Gary Nolan was withdrawing from the All-Star team. He had a sore arm.

Ten days earlier Gary Nolan had covered first base on a ground ball. A base runner was at second. Nolan, running full speed toward the right-field wall took the throw in time for the out. But the runner at third did not stop. He kept coming for the plate. Off-balance, Gary Nolan wheeled and threw home. Something popped. He didn't know it then but at that very moment his career hung in the balance.

The arm became sore. Then sorer. Then it hurt so badly he couldn't throw.

The summer turned into the fall. It was almost playoff time. Nolan wanted to pitch. He was willing to pitch. Yes, there was pain. He could take it. The Reds decided to give him a try. On September 8, he started a game against San Diego. He pitched one inning and was lifted trailing 2-0.

And he steamed. He had words with Sparky Anderson. He was fed up hearing that he had a low pain threshold, that he was babying himself.

"Don't give me any of that pitching with pain," he snapped. "Every pitcher pitches with pain. I've gone out there with my foot torn apart and bleeding. They'll tell you about the pitcher who goes out there with tears in his eyes because it hurts so much. Well, all I can say is that the pain can't be affecting his pitching. No one knows how much you hurt except yourself. No one can know. I would not be sitting here if it didn't hurt bad. You pitch with pain in your arm."

And what did Anderson say? "He'll pitch again when he comes and tells me he's ready to go nine innings."

X-rays, you see, had been negative. Nolan was examined by a San Francisco specialist. His diagnosis was that

Nolan's arm troubles weren't serious or threatening any permanent damage. The Reds, having no clinical evidence to back up Nolan's sore arm claim, would not believe him.

In late September the Reds went through their routine physical examination. X-rays of Nolan's teeth turned up an abcess.

Ah, they said, that is the answer. They had the abcessed tooth extracted. Was that truly the reason or merely a bluff on the Reds' part? Were they thinking Nolan's trouble was mental and that by doing something to help it would give him peace of mind and, therefore, freedom in his arm?

Not long after the story broke that Nolan's troubles were caused by an abcessed tooth did Peter C. Goulding, director of communications for the American Dental Association, speak up."To the contrary, most medical knowledge would point to a conclusion that an abcessed tooth is not likely to cause arm soreness," he said. In other words it was a psych job by the Reds not based on medical knowledge.

Whatever, Gary Nolan put his arm together enough to pitch. He pitched one game in the playoffs and pitched masterfully, going six innings against the hard-hitting Pirates and holding them to four hits and one run. After Nolan left, the Reds lost the game.

"This," he said, his eyes glued to the locker room floor, "is the most disappointment I've ever had in my life. I feel like I let the guys down, like I let my family down. Most of all I feel like I let myself down. You wait all year for something, then it comes and oh, boy, I'll tell you. It's kinda tough to take."

Nolan had pitched well but hadn't completed the game. He was to get another chance. Through the miracle of a Johnny Bench home run off Dave Giusti and a Bob Moose wild pitch that scored George Foster, the Reds won the playoffs and went into the World Series.

Again, Nolan got it together. He pitched two games, a total of eleven innings, giving up just seven hits and four runs. He lost one game. The Reds lost the series in seven. For Gary Nolan, though, the worst was yet to come. The 1973 season came and Gary Nolan had a sore arm. It lasted all year. He pitched only two games the entire season, losing his only decision.

Doctors X-rayed him and stuck him and jabbed him and examined him and still found no clinical evidence of damage. The season ended and the Reds had a new idea for Gary Nolan. The trouble, it was reasoned, had to be nerve damage. They went about treating that, inserting an electrified needle into the arm to kill the sensory nerve they felt was causing the trouble. He already had missed a year. The treatment had to work. Gary Nolan had been tortured enough.

"It was the loneliest position anyone could be in," he recalls. "I wanted to do well. I tried my best. I just couldn't."

He heard the whispers that he wasn't really hurt, that the pain wasn't as bad as he made it.

"I'd hear people say they could imagine what it was like. But they can't. Unless you go through something like this you can't possibly imagine what it's like. I wasn't holding back. I just couldn't do it.

"I know what I went through. I know the pain. I can pitch with pain. It's something I've always done. I just couldn't pitch last year. I only hope I can pitch this year."

This year was 1974. Spring training came. It soon was evident that the electrified needle had produced little in the way of improvement. Some days he could throw, producing optimism among the Reds. It also produced the same reaction on the days when the pain was too intense to throw: "Well, he threw one day, why not the next? It must be in his head."

Two weeks into spring training Nolan had had enough.

"A sharp pain," he said. "Every pitch. It just makes you want to cry. If it was only some of the pitches I could take it. But every pitch." He knew something was in there. He knew the suffering. He begged for help.

"I want help and I want it now. I don't want to wait two or three days. I don't want more tests run on me that were run before. I want to find out what's going on and get it over with."

Gary Nolan was lost. At twenty-five, his career hung in the balance. "I feel," he said, "as if I'm in the middle of the Ohio River in a boat with a hole in it. I can't even throw along the sidelines. When I do I'm just lobbing the ball. My arm hurts so much I don't even want to go to the mound. And I love to pitch."

The decision was made. There was only one last hope of saving the most promising of careers and that was a long shot. Surgery. It would put him out of action again for all of the 1974 season. Two years inactive. And the knife, slicing away into the vital muscles of the shoulders. It was risky but it was all that was left.

"I'll do anything to pitch again," said Nolan.

Nolan was sent to Los Angeles to Dr. Frank Jobe, considered the finest orthopedic specialist in the country. Dr. Jobe examined Nolan.

"How bad is it?" asked Nolan.

"The only way left to help it is surgery," answered the doctor. Nolan expected that. X-rays, taken at a different angle and in a different position than any previous X-rays, revealed a calcium deposit in the shoulder.

"I don't want any ifs, ands, or buts," said Nolan. "What are my chances?"

"It will be touch and go," said Dr. Jobe, "but with work I think you will make it."

On May 13 Dr. Frank Jobe, cutting carefully to avoid the major muscles that go into throwing a pitch, sliced into the pitching arm of Gary Nolan. Looking around inside ("Right at the spot where I pointed with my finger," Nolan was to say, as if to point out that the pain was real, not imaginary,) Dr. Jobe found the culprit. It was a three-quarter inch bone spur, needle like in shape. It had been tormenting the tendons and tissues of the right arm, gouging the muscle.

"Gary Nolan," said Dr. Frank Jobe, "had to have a very high pain threshold to pitch at all with that in his arm." The operation was proclaimed a success but the question now loomed larger than ever. Could Gary Nolan pitch again and could he win in the big leagues? Only time would tell. For six weeks he could do nothing with the arm and it was driving him crazy.

"I never realized how much I really wanted to play baseball until then," said Nolan. He'd sit in front of the television, his wife, Carol, speaking to him or one of the four children coming up to talk and he'd hear nothing. "Mannix would be on and I'd sit there staring at the television and never know how the show ended," he recalls.

At first there was pain in the arm as predicted by Dr. Jobe. But the pain subsided. Six weeks passed and Gary Nolan found himself out playing catch with his sons, Gary and Tim. It was uncomfortable to throw, the muscles weakened by inactivity and a surgeon's scalpel. But time heals all and the arm kept getting stronger and stronger.

Gary Nolan went to the Winter Instructional League, a

veteran among rookies, and worked on the arm. He did nothing spectacular unless throwing without pain is spectacular. The arm got stronger. Winter of '74 disappeared and became spring of '75. It was snowing somewhere up north, but The Big Red Machine was in Tampa, Florida.

Most of the men Gary Nolan broke into baseball with were gone and here he was coming back. To Gary Nolan this spring was not for fun. It was to work and work he did, his confidence bubbling over.

"I believe I'm gonna do it," he said as camp opened, his arm still not tested. "There's no reason why I won't be as good as ever. I think I can win my fifteen or twenty games."

Talk, though, is cheap. Gary Nolan had to talk with his arm. Slowly, ever so slowly, did he take it. But the more he threw the more relaxed he became. No pain. If there was no pain Gary Nolan could win in the big leagues. He'd already proved that.

"If Nolan can pitch it's like getting a free Catfish Hunter," said Sparky Anderson, Hunter having been in the headlines for signing a $3.8 million contract with the New York Yankees after being declared a free agent because Charles O. Finley, the Oakland owner, had failed to live up to his contract.

The fact of the matter was that the Reds were in dire need of Nolan. The year before without Nolan they had finished behind Los Angeles in the West and the Cincinnati starting pitching was questionable. A healthy, winning Nolan was the answer if it could become a reality.

Finally, the day everyone had been waiting for arrived. March 14, 1975, Gary Nolan took the mound for the Cincinnati Reds in his first exhibition game. The scene was Al Lopez Field in Tampa, the same field on which that eighteen-year-old kid out of the bushes had boldly pitched himself into the big leagues.

All spring the reporters had come to Gary Nolan over and over with the same questions. Could he come back? Had the surgery worked? Was his fast ball of a big league nature?

"It's beginning to bug me," Nolan admitted.

He went to the mound on that Thursday afternoon and as they played the National Anthem his heart beat out a steady rhythm under the familiar Cincinnati uniform with the Number 38.

"How long does this thing last?" he asked himself, the eighty-two-degree heat beating down on him. The opposition was the Minnesota Twins.

Nolan's mind was churning away. For some reason, just briefly, he recalled walking out the door that morning. He got a goodbye kiss from his wife, Carol, and the four children.

"No matter how good or bad I am I'll be giving it my all," he told his wife.

The feeling was strange, standing there on that minor league diamond with 2,500 people in the stands. "I don't want to embarrass myself," was all he could think of. "You've got to have good control. Don't kick any ground balls. You're back home."

It was game time and Gary Nolan, with that deceptively easy windup, delivered his first pitch. It was a high fast ball and it carried a message. "I can and will throw the fast ball," it seemed to say.

Scouts in the stands—and there were plenty of them, all attracted to see the comeback of Gary Nolan—looked at each other in amazement. Not at all a bad fast ball. Good enough to get by. And it's early. He's still got seven weeks to get stronger.

Three innings. That's as far as Nolan went. The Twins touched him for two hits, nothing else. He walked no one. It was as if he'd never been away. The performance was outstanding with Nolan expressing that he could have pitched longer and harder with better control.

"The thing that keeps me going," he said, "is that I have to show people I can come back . . . show them the kind of person I am."

And come back he did. Ten days later against Boston he pitched seven innings, the first Red to go that far in the spring. Already the Reds had given up worrying about Gary Nolan's arm. That was healthy. Now they went to work on making him a pitcher again. The layoff had led him into some bad habits and they sent back to Cincinnati for videotapes of the Gary Nolan of 1970 and 1971 to show him what he was doing wrong.

Still, he was getting hitters out.

"That's a funny thing," said Larry Shepard, the Reds' pitching coach. "There is such a thing as charisma with a big league pitcher who has been a success. They get people out. No matter what, no matter how hard the ball is hit it's right at someone. I remember when we ran him out against Houston one day a couple of years ago—when the arm was bad—and he threw nothing. All he did was pitch six innings of one-hit ball."

After that game Leo Durocher, then manager of the Astros, was shocked at Nolan's success. "I wanted to grab a bat and go out and hit against him myself," said Durocher.

Gary Nolan was tricking people. His fast ball was enough to keep them off stride, his change-up as elusive as ever and his curve breaking sharply. Twice during the spring he was hit hard but it never discouraged him.

124

On April 4 he finished off spring training by going seven innings against Detroit, allowing one run and five hits. He said he could have gone all the way. He was ready for the season, the season when The Big Red Machine would put it all together and when Gary Nolan would return.

Gary Nolan made his regular season debut in San Diego in the fifth game of the season. And he summed it up after it was over: "I pitched too good to lose." But lose he did, 3-2. Six innings, three runs, no walks. He was impressive.

"Three or four more starts and Gary Nolan will be the best pitcher in the National League," gushed Anderson. That didn't happen. But Gary Nolan, a healthy Gary Nolan, was a winner and that more than anything solidified the Cincinnati pitching staff, made it respectable. And the future was ahead. Gary Nolan with all he'd been through still was just twenty-seven years old.

"I should just be reaching my prime," he said.

7

JOHNNY AND VICKIE

It had all come so fast for Johnny Bench. The fame, the glory, being the idol of millions, and the money. It had come maybe too fast. After all, it is hard for a farm boy from the sticks of Oklahoma to put his feet on the ground when he is riding on the shoulders of the world.

It had happened to Mickey Mantle, who was Johnny Bench's boyhood idol. For Mantle it was even worse than for Bench. Mantle was supposed to be the new Joe DiMaggio. He had to contend with New York. And he was basically a shy person.

Johnny Bench had to contend with no ghost of the past. Johnny Bench had Cincinnati, not New York, with which to contend. And Johnny Bench was an outgoing sort of person. Even in his earliest days he presented a picture of maturity. But this was an outward picture. Inside, there was the heart of the young boy.

Johnny Bench used to joke about his early beginnings.

"Binger, Oklahoma," he would say, "is a mile and a half past 'Resume Speed.'"

It was a small town and Johnny Bench, part Indian and frequently taunted about it, spent days picking cotton and peanuts out in the field. He also spent days becoming a legend in the area, so much so that they all started claiming him — Midwest City, Oklahoma City, Anadarko, and Binger, which was his home.

In high school he was a pitcher. Not a bad one either as evidenced by a 75-3 record. He was an all-state basketball player. He was the total athlete.

As hard as it may be to believe, Johnny Bench was not a first-round draft choice. The Cincinnati Reds in 1965, the first year of the free agent draft, selected Bernie Carbo ahead of him. The trouble was no one had really seen Bench catch.

In the second round Johnny Bench was picked. The Reds, having held a tryout in Binger, had asked Bench to throw from behind the plate in infield practice. He did that, then went out and pitched a game and won.

The Reds liked what they saw but they never could have guessed just what they had on their hands. It wasn't long, though, before they knew as did the world.

In 1966, Johnny Bench's second year in professional baseball, he played at Peninsula. He appeared in just ninety-eight games yet hit twenty-two home runs. At age nineteen, his uniform number was retired. By the end of 1967 he had a trial with the Cincinnati Reds. He was stuck behind the plate, managed somehow to break a finger and it was to be a blessing. By breaking the finger he narrowly missed playing too many games to qualify as a rookie in 1968.

Given the catching job in 1968 over three veterans — Johnny Edwards, Don Pavletich, and Jim Coker — by Dave Bristol, Bench was named Rookie of the Year. Honors, though, were nothing new. He had already been named Minor League Player of the Year. Success was coming quickly to Johnny Bench. Even before he had taken over as the regular catcher of the Reds his picture had appeared on the cover of *Sports Illustrated.* It was one of the few times the *Sports Illustrated* cover did not prove to be a jinx.

Great things were happening to Johnny Bench. For the first time in his life money was coming to him. He was handsome and single. This was working in his favor. He was the new Cincinnati hero, taking over from Pete Rose just as Jack Nicklaus had burst onto the professional golf tour to challenge Arnold Palmer, causing a split between those two.

There was no split between Bench and Rose. Rose did all he could to help his new rival for the love of the masses. He took Bench under his wing, went into business with him.

"The thing I liked best about Johnny Bench was that he moved to Cincinnati right away, made it his home. So many guys star in a town during the baseball season then head out when the season ends," said Rose, who loves Cincinnati as deeply as it loves him.

When the Tulsa *World* newspaper held a banquet in Bench's honor he sat there calmly listening to greats from all walks of life sing his praise. Finally it was his turn to speak.

"You all have forgotten to introduce a great man who is sitting in the audience," said Johnny Bench. "My father — Ted Bench."

Ted Bench rose to his feet, tears running down his cheeks.

"My, what a man," thought the world. But all was not as it appeared. There was still the child in Bench. It was a different woman every night, perhaps trying to make up for lost time spent in Binger when he had no money, no fame, when only sports interested him. Perhaps it was his fatalistic outlook on life.

In those early years Johnny Bench cared only about Johnny Bench. He had set his goals. He wanted to become a millionaire. He did not want to play baseball past age thirty-two. He had a taste of show business when Bob Hope took him on one of his Christmas tours of Viet Nam.

Johnny Bench began dating one of the Ding-A-Ling Sisters. He began dating Miss Kansas. He had his own television show. He appeared on "Mission: Impossible." He became friendly with Bobby Goldsboro, Charley Pride, Chuck Connors. He played in Bob Hope's golf tournament. You put a microphone in front of Johnny Bench and he became the interviewer, not you.

In 1970, he became the youngest man ever to be named the National League's Most Valuable Player, having a spectacular season with forty-five home runs and 148 runs batted in. The forty-five homers were the most ever hit by a right-handed Cincinnati batter. The 148 runs batted in were the most ever driven in by any Cincinnati batter. Johnny Bench at this time was the biggest thing in baseball. He was the swinging bachelor, Joe Namath without sophistication.

But he was about to begin growing up.

For the first time in his life he was to taste defeat as an

athlete. The Reds of '71 fell apart. After having won the pennant so easily the year before, they tumbled to a fourth-place tie. They fell below .500. And Johnny Bench was to hit just .238 with twenty-seven home runs and sixty-one runs batted in.

They booed him in Cincinnati. He found it hard to take. The following spring he announced that he would no longer tip his cap to the fans after hitting a homer. It was a threat that didn't last because in 1972 he bounced back. He was the MVP again, the home run champion again, the RBI champion again. And the Reds were National League champions again.

They were champions because Johnny Bench had hit one of the most dramatic home runs in Cincinnati history, a ninth-inning right-field homer off Dave Giusti of Pittsburgh to tie the final playoff game, a game the Reds were to win minutes later when George Foster scored from third base on Bob Moose's wild pitch.

Suddenly he was again a hero. Then came the news. In early December, 1972, the Cincinnati Reds made the announcement. It startled the world. During a routine physical examination a spot had been detected on Johnny Bench's right lung. Surgery was necessary to determine the seriousness of the ailment. The worst wasn't ever really said but it was thought. Johnny Bench at age twenty-five could have lung cancer.

They prayed for Johnny Bench in Cincinnati and around the world as Dr. Luis Gonzalez opened his chest, removed a rib and cut into the lung. The lesion was there all right. It was benign. They breathed a sigh of relief for Johnny Bench. Nothing more than a fungus had entered Bench's lung.

How, they thought, had he done it? He had learned before the National League playoffs in which he was to hit the dramatic home run, before the World Series, of the spot on the lung and he had played, keeping it a secret from virtually everyone.

It was his second brush with death, having been involved in a school bus collision as a youngster, banging up his shoulder and saving the life of another on the bus when he threw his body on top of him as the bus crashed.

There was a certain fatalism in Johnny Bench's life. Now, he was changing. The operation, the cancer scare, had shown him there was more to life than just baseball. There was more to life than winning and losing and accumulating piles of land and money.

So in 1973 they booed Johnny Bench as he fought off the aftereffects of the operation. He had an off year for the man who everyone had already put into baseball's Hall of Fame, hitting just .253 with twenty-five home runs.

"Off year?" asked Bench. "I didn't know if ever I would be able to play again. I drove in 101 runs. It was no off year."

By 1974 the only reminder of the operation was a welted scar that ran from front to back around the chest. He was strong again and hit thirty-three home runs and drove in a league-high 129 runs, his third RBI title.

More than that, he was now mature.

At the end of the 1974 season he confided to friends that before spring training he would be married. He said this knowing he had not yet found the right girl.

In late December Johnny Bench called a friend in Orlando, Florida and asked for the phone number of a pretty model. The number given Johnny Bench was in New

York. It was the phone number of one Vickie Chesser. Bench made the call. They spoke for ten or fifteen minutes. He then asked if she was busy over New Year's. Vickie assured Johnny Bench she was not.

"Well, then, how would you like to spend New Year's weekend in Las Vegas with me? I'll provide you with a plane ticket and a room of your own," said Bench.

"You're bananas," Vickie Chesser answered. "But so am I. I'll go."

It was set. On December 28 Vickie Chesser flew to Cincinnati to join Bench at the wedding of Bill Spiegel, a local television program director.

"I didn't even know what Johnny looked like," Vickie Chesser admitted. "I never had time to check what he looked like."

When Vickie Chesser arrived at the airport she wasn't sure what to expect. Bench had described himself to her as "more like a football player than a baseball player," in hopes of making their meeting easier.

"At the airport I wasn't sure the man I saw was Johnny, so I turned around and started the other way, then came back," explained Vickie.

"Is it that bad?" asked Bench. It wasn't.

While Vickie didn't know what she was getting into, Johnny Bench did. He had looked up photos of her. Vickie Chesser may not have known what Johnny Bench looked like but she knew he was just no ordinary baseball player. After agreeing to the date she called her father, Clyde E. Chesser, a retired Navy man, and asked him about Johnny Bench.

"My dad doesn't get very exuberant or excited," she said. "He just said, 'He's probably the best ballplayer going today.'"

At the time, Vicki Chesser was dating another man, "a professional football player," who she has steadfastly refused to name. "I'd been advised that most jocks are creeps but the person who told me that also said Johnny was an exception," said Vickie.

They flew to Las Vegas bringing along Johnny's mother and father. It was a fun weekend for Bench and maybe even more so for the twenty-five-year-old model out of Mt. Pleasant, South Carolina and the University of South Carolina.

Almost immediately Johnny Bench was serious. Upon returning home from Las Vegas he was telling people he'd met the girl he was going to marry.

"I was scared to death of marriage," Vickie recalls. "But he was so sure, even a couple of weeks before I was." Vickie Chesser decided to test Johnny Bench. "I can't cook," she told him.

"All right with me," answered Bench. "We can eat in my restaurant. The food is super."

It was a decision Vickie had to make. Johnny Bench was sure. She wasn't. Although a small town girl, she had fallen in love with New York City.

"The theater, I loved it," she said. "And every morning, real early, I'd get up and jog with a friend. It was beautiful. We'd get to see New York when everyone was asleep and the sun was coming up and reflecting off the buildings."

Johnny Bench saw Vickie Chesser time after time. He went to Mt. Pleasant to meet her parents. He called her every day. She was convinced. She had found her man. "I would have gone to a desert isle with Johnny Bench," she said. "When I found what this guy was doing with the little time he has to himself, visiting children in hospitals, children with leukemia and things like that, I decided he can't be all bad."

In true Johnny Bench fashion, on January 20, a Monday, just three weeks after they had first met he went on television and announced his engagement to Vickie Chesser.

The city was taken by surprise. Johnny Bench was going to marry. Who was this young lady, everyone asked? Then they found out. They had seen her on television; seen her doing a toothpaste commercial—a commercial that fittingly enough began with the line, "How's your love life?"

The wedding was set for February 21. It was to be the social event of the decade in Cincinnati. A list of 900 invitations went out, even including one to President Gerald Ford. Bench's public relations flacks had been working hard inviting the famous and the near famous.

The newspapers played it like a royal wedding. There will be 650 pounds of roast beef, one hundred pounds of roast ham, 1,200 egg rolls, one hundred pounds of cooked shrimp, 4,000 mixed drinks, and a five-foot high wedding cake weighing a hundred pounds and costing between $300 and $400, it was reported.

On Friday, February 21, as the Cincinnati Reds were beginning to gather in Florida for spring training which opened the next day, Johnny Bench and Vickie Chesser walked down the aisle at Christ Church, answering the questions of Rector Edward Sims by saying, "I will, by God's help."

Within a day, though, the joy of marriage was lessened by a tragedy. Young Phillip Buckingham, whose friendship with Bench had become known around the world, lost his battle to leukemia, the spunky, curly-haired five-year-old dying in Barney's Children's Hospital in Dayton, Ohio. The

134

relationship between Bench and Phillip Buckingham had started in November, 1973. On a department store promotion in Dayton, Bench learned of the youngster's illness and his fondness for the Cincinnati superstar.

"Phillip Buckingham," said Bench, "changed my life."

That first Christmas, Bench came to the Buckingham home with gifts for Phillip and his family. At the same time a Dayton car dealer gave the family a car so it would be easier to get Phillip to the hospital for medication. In 1974, Bench dedicated his first home run of the season to Phillip.

Phillip Buckingham had an invitation to attend the wedding of Johnny Bench. He was too ill to go. But Bench had promised to save him a piece of wedding cake. The cake was never eaten. Phillip Buckingham was dead and Johnny Bench's life was saddened no small amount.

The Bench's spent their "honeymoon" in spring training, she becoming accustomed to the life of a baseball wife and he becoming accustomed to being a husband.

By mid-March, there was more tragedy. Jim McGlothlin, a former Cincinnati pitcher, was stricken with what was thought to be cancer. He had been hospitalized, given just days to live, then miraculously survived. The father of three small children—one of them adopted—McGlothlin had no medical insurance and his hospital bills had grown to nearly $20,000. He had no way to pay them. Johnny Bench stepped in. Along with Pete Rose and country singer Jon Potter, they prepared a benefit for McGlothlin.

The spring moved on, Johnny Bench enjoying the greatest spring of his career. Opening day came and went. The Reds got off slowly. Johnny Bench got off slowly. He was booed and there were whispers all over that married life was not helping Johnny Bench.

On April 22 the Reds were playing the San Francisco Giants. Gary Matthews was at second base when Chris Speier rifled a single to left field. Pete Rose fielded the ball and fired to the plate. Bench had the base path blocked off, the ball and Matthews arriving simultaneously. There was a terrible collision. Matthews was safe. Bench's shoulder began to throb.

"A bruise," was the diagnosis. The shoulder continued to ache. X-rays were negative.

April became May, May became June, June became July. In July, Johnny Bench was named to head a campaign of the American Cancer Society known as Athletes Against Cancer. He was the man for the job, his own scare and the death of Phillip Buckingham making the disease very real to him.

And still the shoulder ached. X-rays continued to show nothing. The only relief he got was from cortisone shots that probed deeply into the joint. While he was hitting well he had no power. At times he could not raise the left arm above his shoulder, unable to take his uniform off without help. He continued to play even though Sparky Anderson said he was planning to rest him.

Bench first thought he had separated the shoulder. Then he believed he had arthritis. In late August it got to be too much for him. He went to a Chicago orthopedic specialist who diagnosed a damaged cartilage in the shoulder joint. Fluid was drained. Rest was prescribed. And Bench spoke of what he was going through.

"This has been torture," he said. "I've been trying to contribute, to help the team win, but I've feared that I might damage the shoulder more. And if it was hurting my career it wasn't worth it." The rest wasn't to come even though the championship had been cinched. September came and Bench continued to play.

On September 13, a Fred Norman pitch in the dirt hit Bench in the ankle. He finished the game. The next morning, though, he could hardly stand, the ankle badly swollen. He went to a doctor in San Francisco.

X-rays were taken. They were negative unless you want to count three old fractures they showed that had never been discovered. Three times in the past Bench had broken a bone in his foot without having it treated.

He was on crutches, though, and looked like the rest he needed would be his. No way. The ankle healed quickly. Within five days he was back in the starting lineup. The shoulder still ached. And more was to come. In the third inning, fielding a bunt, he pulled his groin muscle. He was doubtful for the playoffs and he was bitter. He wasn't going to be rushed back into the lineup.

"I don't care if I play another game this season. If it hurts, I'm not playing until the playoffs. I'm not going to jeopardize my career," he said. He returned for the final three games of the regular season. He played through the playoffs and the World Series. And he thought about the coming year, about the pain he had experienced in 1975. What was left to drive him to endure it again, having money, fame, a world's championship?

"Probably very little is left to drive me," he said. "If it aches like it did this year I would probably take as long as is needed to get it cured, no matter what they wanted (they being management that knows Bench is vital to the team and to the gate).

"I wouldn't go through it again. I'd find me a doctor. I'd find me enough specialists and everything. I'd check with everyone until I found out what was wrong and corrected it. I wouldn't care if it meant not playing or anything else. It wouldn't bother me."

Johnny Bench had, indeed, become a changed man. He had become a person instead of a machine. He had learned that there is a world out there beyond the concrete walls of a stadium.

The Burial of the Dodgers

By early July it was over. The 1975 Western Division pennant race belonged to The Big Red Machine. Not that the standings were that one-sided by this time, the Reds winning on July 5 to go ahead by eight games. That wasn't it. It was more a matter of attitude.

Morgan's opening day observation—"they can't think they're better than we are"—was proving to be so true. For the Reds it was fun. They were laughing all the way. For the Dodgers it was disaster.

Steve Garvey, the All-American boy, had become the center of a controversy that was threatening to split the Dodgers apart. His teammates had accused him in print of being too much of a "goody-goody." Imagine signing autographs, going to hospitals to visit sick children, being a goodwill ambassador for baseball.

As the Dodgers fought, the Reds laughed. In San Diego, the Reds won, as outfielder Gene Locklear turned left field into an unplayable lie. Pete Rose called Locklear, a close friend of his and the man whose paintings hang in Rose's pancake house in Cincinnati, "Pele."

"He kicks the ball around the outfield so much he looks like Pele," said Rose.

And Fred Norman, after wildness plagued him a game, commented: "I was pitching around everyone. Even my catcher, Johnny Bench."

The winners tell jokes and the losers cry "deal." The Dodgers were crying. On July 6, the Reds won 13-2 despite three errors in four innings by Joe Morgan, the sure-handed Gold Glove winner at second base. "He pulled off the hat trick," laughed Bench.

On July 7 Tony Perez, now the hottest of the Red Hots, hit a most memorable home run, the baseball carrying into the red seats—the uppermost seats—in Riverfront Stadium. That area had not been reached since 1971, the red seats being some fifty feet above field level and 330 feet directly down the line in left.

Perez was the first man ever to reach the red seats, having done it in 1970, the first year of Riverfront Stadium. Now he had done it again, the only player to reach the upper deck twice in the brief history of Riverfront Stadium.

The Reds kept winning. It was almost time for the All-Star game. The starting lineups for the game were named, the Reds placing Rose, Morgan, Concepcion, and Bench on the team.

Later it was announced that Perez had been named to the team and Perez reacted in his own inimitable fashion. "I not really belong. But I take it. The fans vote for me. At least I know someone likes me," he said. Although Perez' batting average stood at just .250, it had to be recalled that on May 15 he was at but .194. In two months he had gained fifty-six points.

While the Reds were thrilled with Perez' selection to the All-Star team, they were less than thrilled by Dodger manager Walter Alston's announcement that his own relief pitcher, Mike Marshall, was a National League All-Star.

This selection, an obvious gesture by Alston to please his record-breaking relief pitcher who already had demanded and received clauses in his contract that gave him a suite on the road complete, when possible, with a water bed, infuriated the Reds. Marshall at the time was 3-5 and had been injured a good part of the first half of the season. His earned run average stood at 3.00.

By way of comparison Jack Billingham, who was 10-3, did not make the team. Neither did Cincinnati reliever Will McEnaney, 3-1, with a 1.38 earned run average and eight saves as compared to five for Marshall. "A farce," is the way Billingham termed it.

"He's not having any All-Star season," added McEnaney.

"The reason he picked Marshall is that he thought Marshall would cry and wouldn't pitch good for him," charged Billingham.

"They can have the All-Star game. We'll take The Fall Classic," prophesied McEnaney.

The Reds continued to win. Trailing 7-4 in the eighth inning against Philadelphia, they scored five runs and won, 9-7. "There ain't no way we can lose this thing no more," crowed Anderson. "We can only give it away."

And Philadelphia's superstar left-fielder Greg Luzinski chipped in: "I'm just glad to get out of here."

The last day before the All-Star break saw the Reds going against Tom Seaver. Seaver was 13-4 at the moment with a microscopic 1.79 earned run average. The Reds beat him 5-3. They had won ten in a row and were twelve-and-a-half on top.

The Big Red Machine was already beginning to look ahead to the playoffs, to the World Series. They were sure the division belonged to them, becoming even surer when, the day after the All-Star game, Dodger second baseman Davey Lopes opened his mouth.

"We've been destroyed psychologically by the way the Reds have been playing," Lopes said. The Reds giggled to themselves . . . The All-Star game had come and gone, Rose probably deserving the Most Valuable Player nod that went to Chicago's Bill Madlock and the Mets' Jon Matlack. Rose had netted two singles and a sacrifice fly. "I thought Rose was a cinch to win it," said Anderson, disappointed that his own didn't win the honor.

The winning streak ended the day after the All-Star break, Montreal's Steve Rogers shutting Cincinnati out. So the next day Perez hit a grand-slam homer and the Reds waltzed 10-3.

"I hit them farther, but never any that scored any more runs," joked Perez, whose first big league home run had also been a grand slam.

Everything was going the way of the Reds. Their superstars were playing like — well, playing like superstars.

Morgan was new to the superstar status. Oh, he had long been paid like a superstar but on a team with Rose, Bench, and Perez he had been somewhat overlooked. Now, in the midst of his greatest season he was learning there was more to stardom than just running to the bank.

"I'm no different than I ever was except for my batting average," he offered. But people refused to believe him. They were calling him "the best player in baseball," a phrase usually reserved for Johnny Bench.

"I always felt I was an all-around player. I take pride in being able to do a lot of things. I'm not doing anything I didn't do before except hit for average," he swore. But what an average he had, .340, third in the league. It was a long way from the .273 career average he had put together.

Joe Morgan, playing for a first-place team, having a season that defied description, liked to think of himself as a private person. But he was having trouble remaining private. The phone rang constantly, usually people he didn't even know.

"They just want to talk," he explained.

One day it would be a Philadelphia fan. "You gave me an autographed baseball in Connie Mack Stadium a few years ago. I just wanted to say thank you," the nameless, faceless voice would say.

"I can't go down to eat àny more on the road. They swarm on me. Now I just sit up in my room and order room service and listen to my music and read."

Mostly, Joe Morgan read adventure comic books. A college student during the off-season, he read the books to take his mind off it all, off the pressure of the pennant race and the pressure of being a star. Every once in a while he ventured into the coffee shop. It always seemed to happen this way.

A person would sit down with him. He had never seen the other person before. The person sat and talked uninvited, and not taking any hints that Joe Morgan would like to be left alone. So, politely, Joe Morgan talked and ate in a hurry. Joe Morgan prefers to be alone with his music and the relaxation it brings with it. He listens mostly to jazz and soul music. Keeping in character he tries to keep his family separated from the spotlight.

"My wife, Gloria," he says, "I want her to be a mother and a housewife, not get involved in the game." And Gloria understands, staying out of the limelight in the background, not wanting any part of the life fame has brought the likes of Morgan, Bench, Perez, and Rose.

The Dodgers came to town in late July. The tickets had

been sold for some time, the faithful fans of Cincinnati expecting a real shoot-out. Now, no one cared. The Reds led by twelve and a half. The Dodgers were a beaten bunch, only Garvey seeming to have anything resembling faith, he being engrossed in reading *The Miracle of Coogan's Bluff*, the story of the New York Giants' late run at the Brooklyn Dodgers that produced a pennant on Bobby Thomson's home run.

The Reds were gunning for Mike Marshall. They wanted to prove him to be less than an All-Star. In the first game of the series-opening doubleheader, though, Marshall was king, retiring Rose for the final out in a 4-3 Dodger victory. So the second game came along. Again it was Rose vs. Marshall. This time Rose hit a three-run, eighth-inning homer to produce a 6-3 Cincinnati victory.

"He won the first game. It was my turn to win," snapped Rose.

A day later Pete Rose had four hits and scored three runs as the Reds won 5-3. The best the Dodgers could do in this series that they had to sweep was to split it. They could gain no ground on first place and the man who had destroyed them was Pete Rose.

A year earlier when the Dodgers won the pennant Rose had destroyed the Reds. He had hit but .158 against the Dodgers and, in Dodger Stadium with the crowd throwing things at him and burying him in obscenities, he had but three hits in thirty-nine tries.

It got so bad that for the first time in his career Rose said, "playing baseball isn't any fun." He said it after he had gone hitless against L.A., had caught a fly ball as a chunk of ice flew past his ear, as the bleacher fans cursed his mother. Now, revenge was his and he could revel in his own heroics.

While Rose was torrid Morgan was slumping. He had just ended an 0-for-18 slump. Now, the Dodger series history, he sat in front of his locker and spoke. "Maybe," moaned Joe Morgan, "I do too much for a little guy. I almost blew the whole season with this. I'm tired. I'm always battling but I'm going to rest somewhere."

Similar statements on another team would have gone as a criticism of the manager for not giving Morgan a rest. With the Reds they just were fuel for "the boys." The next day when Morgan showed up at the clubhouse, a pillow and sleeping bag had been set in front of his locker. There was a cup of coffee, a pair of slippers, and two aspirin tablets.

"You guys are crazy, insane," shouted Morgan. "I love it. Without this I'd hang myself."

Bench and Perez had struck. It was the kind of thing that typified The Big Red Machine. "Of all the reasons we are succeeding, the most important is that not one of our stars has ever lost his coconut," explains Anderson. "Our big players are big people as well. They've never given me, the coaches, or the organization, any problems. They've never become prima donnas and they won't tolerate anyone else becoming one."

The Reds were riding high. They were also looking for a challenge. The Dodgers had proven themselves to be unworthy of the challenge in 1975. As July turned into August the challenge the Reds were seeking emerged in a brash, right-handed rookie pitcher.

San Francisco's John Montefusco had just defeated the Chicago Cubs 10-2. The perspiration had not yet dried on his forehead when he began flapping his lip. A likable, almost lovable kid Montefusco was making a name for himself by being the brashest thing to hit the big league since Dizzy Dean.

144

"My next start is against Cincinnati and I'm gonna shut them out. I did it last year when they had a better club and I struck out Johnny Bench three times. This year I figure they're not as good so I'll shut 'em out again and strike Bench out four times," predicted the man they called The Count of Montefusco.

Montefusco was a total put-on. Confident, yes, but he was not that confident. He was just trying to take a shortcut to fame, the same one Muhammad Ali had taken.

"I like to look in the newspaper and see who I'm pitching against next. I like to know who's gonna get the loss," crowed Montefusco.

Al Michaels, the Giants' radio announcer, had fallen in love with Montefusco. It all came about early in the season when Montefusco approached Michaels.

"These guys on the team are all too young for me to hang around with," said the twenty-five-year-old Count. "I'm gonna start hanging around with you."

"Before you do," answered Michaels, "you're gonna have to do something like pitch a couple of shutouts." End of conversation. Montefusco pitched again and sure enough he threw a shutout. Five minutes after the game the phone in the broadcasting booth rang. The voice on the other end belonged to Montefusco.

"That's one," he said simply, hanging up the phone.

When Montefusco went against the Reds he was 10-4 and on a four-game winning streak. "I'm a streak pitcher. I may never lose again," he boasted.

Then he had to pitch. Montefusco became Monte-fiasco. He didn't beat the Reds as he said he would. He didn't strike Johnny Bench out four times as he said he would. He didn't strike Johnny Bench out at all.

But then he didn't really have much of a chance to,

lasting only an inning and two-thirds as the Reds gave him a lesson in humility. 11-6.

And who should have delivered the knockout blow? None other than Bench who hit his twenty-first homer with two on in the middle of the six-run second inning. The fact of the matter was that the Reds were enjoying Montefusco. Even before the confrontation there was some byplay. Montefusco stood by the batting cage as the Reds took batting practice.

"Morgan's not playing tonight," Bench informed The Count.

"Hmmmm, if Morgan's not playing then it will be a no-hitter," said Montefusco, everyone breaking up in laughter.

When it was over, though, Montefusco wasn't laughing, leaving as the crowd stood and jeered. In response, as only he could, Montefusco doffed his cap and waved it at the crowd as if he were a returning hero. The challenge issued by Montefusco was fun to The Big Red Machine. Not so with the next challenge, that offered by the Dodgers' Don Sutton.

Rule 8.02 (4) in the official rules of baseball reads:

"The pitcher shall not rub the ball on his glove, person or clothing; deface the ball in any manner; deliver what is called the 'shine' ball, 'spit' ball or 'emery' ball."

Going further, the rule, in Paragraph B, states:

"The pitcher shall not have on his person, or in his possession, any foreign substance. For such infraction of this section, the penalty shall be immediate ejection from the game."

This brings up "the great sandpaper controversy of 1975."

To his teammates Sutton is known as "Elmer Gantry." To Sparky Anderson he is "a cheat." Anderson and the Reds believed Sutton had a small piece of sandpaper hidden away in his glove that he was using to "doctor" the baseball.

"Sparky Anderson," said Don Sutton, "is the cryingest manager I've ever seen with a thirteen-and-a-half game lead."

"Don Sutton is a cheating fool," answered Sparky Anderson.

Anderson was certain Sutton was cheating. In Cincinnati Anderson retained fourteen baseballs that were thrown out of play the last time Sutton had pitched against the Reds. None had been hit.

"Each," said Anderson, "had a strange mark in either of two places." Anderson was certain in this game that the same mark would show up on the baseballs. After Bench was called out on strikes Anderson approached Bob Engel, the plate umpire.

"Bob," said Sparky, "was that a new ball Sutton used to strike Bench out with?"

"It was," answered Engel.

"Then I'm gonna tell you where there's a mark on it now," said Anderson.

He told Engel. Engel looked. He found a mark. Engel said nothing to Sutton. Instead, he waited until the sixth inning right after Rose had doubled to left, one of five hits Rose was to get in the game. Sutton knew the search was coming. As early as the third inning he had asked Engel, "Do you want to shake me down now or later?"

It was later. "I was trying to shake him down when he least expected it," said Engel.

Bob Engel searched Don Sutton's glove. He turned it inside out. He found no evidence of sandpaper. There was no proof. So Sutton was allowed to continue in the game. There was only one way to handle such a situation and Bench took it into his own hands. He hit a three-run homer

147

off Sutton. It made the game exciting even though it was meaningless.

All that was left now of the 1975 season were some individual goals of the players and Rose was the first to reach one. With 50,121 in the stands on Sunday, August 17, Rose broke an 0-for-7 string with a line drive single through the middle off Bruce Kison.

The hit was the 2,500th of Rose's thirteen-year career and it helped the Reds sweep the Pittsburgh Pirates, giving them their eighth win in a row and an incredible sixty-two out of eighty-one.

Rose was on his way toward 3,000 hits and a date with the Hall of Fame.

"The Hall of Fame, that's something everyone thinks about. It would be something, to see your name in print, with the words 'Hall of Famer' after it," he said.

But the man who set the most meaningful personal record during the stretch run was a man who wasn't supposed to be around at all—Atanasio Rigal "Tony" Perez. Tony Perez might well have been the biggest bargain in the history of baseball; a million dollar steal for $2.50.

It was April, 1959. Fidel Castro was still holed up in the hills of Cuba. Dwight Eisenhower was President of the United States. And Tony Perez was sixteen years old, living in an area where sugar was king and where you grew up to spend your life chained to the sugar factory.

Tony Perez did not want to spend his days as had his father, farming and working in the factory. He wanted to play baseball. Along came the Cincinnati Reds and they said, "Son, we're gonna make you a ballplayer."

Tony Perez said, "Si."

"They give me nothing," Tony Perez now recalls. "Just two dollars and fifty cents for my visa. I just want to play ball. That is all I ever want to do." Not even a pair of spikes were thrown into the deal, Perez saying, "I buy my own."

Perez turned seventeen and the man from the United States gave him a ticket to fly on this thing called an airplane. "I was scared," he admits, never having been on a plane before. He went to Geneva, New York and began playing baseball, a skinny shortstop. "I no get homesick," he remembers. "I was playing ball and that make me happy."

Tony Perez was in a "D" league, the lowest minor league in baseball at the time. He thought it was heaven. But he soon learned.

"I didn't realize what the big leagues was," he says. Then I watch the big leagues on television and I want to get to the big leagues."

And get there he did, becoming one of the best. On August 26, as the Reds routed Chicago 11-4, Tony Perez became the second man in Cincinnati Reds' history to drive in 1,000 runs. Then on September 2, on a night when the Reds were to win 10-4 over San Diego to drop their magic number for clinching the Western Division to seven, Tony Perez rifled a base hit to left field, Cesar Geronimo coming in to score. The run batted in was the 1,010th of Perez' career, making him the all-time Cincinnati Red leader, surpassing Frank Robinson.

Tony Perez stood at first base as the crowd rose to its feet and passed along its appreciation of the accomplishment of the thirty-three-year-old Cuban. Tony Perez was given the ball as a souvenir. He tossed it to the bat boy who brought it over to the stands. Standing there in the front row was Victor Perez, 9, and Eduardo, 6.

"They were supposed to be home in bed," Tony Perez

explained. "Today was the first day of school. But they tell me they not going to stay home. They say they want the ball and that I'm going to get the RBI tonight."

With the crowd standing and cheering and Victor and Eduardo Perez wearing smiles that were bright enough to light the entire stadium, they took the baseball and presented it to their mother, Pituka Perez, for safekeeping.

Five days later it was over. On September 7, the Cincinnati Reds officially owned their fourth Western Division championship in six years. It ended on a Sunday, the Reds defeating San Francisco 8-4.

Still, they didn't know if they were champions or not. The Dodgers were playing in Atlanta and had to lose for the championship to be cinched. Due to fly to San Diego by charter after the game, the Reds were in no hurry. The champagne was iced. So they waited, the players sitting around in front of their lockers, an eerie quiet over the room. Upstairs in the press box the Reds opened a direct line to Atlanta Stadium to listen as the rain-delayed game began again.

In the press box sat Bob Howsam, the team president, Louis Nippert, the chairman of the board, Dick Wagner, the vice-president, and a couple of public relations people.

The Braves carried a 4-3 lead into the ninth. It didn't hold up. The Dodgers, with a run being walked home, tied the game. But in the bottom of the ninth Marty Perez shot a two-out, bases-loaded single through the middle and the Reds were champions.

"Pop, pop, fizzzz," went the champagne in the locker room.

Then it was time for business. The Reds got on a plane and flew to San Diego. They had to finish out the regular season, prepare for Pittsburgh and the playoffs. They had three weeks of no-pressure baseball ahead of them before the money went back on the line.

Sparky Anderson took the opportunity to rest his regulars, allowing Terry Crowley, Ed Armbrister, Doug Flynn, Bill Plummer, Don Werner, Darrel Chaney, Merv Rettenmund, and Danny Driessen — men who had contributed so much all season coming off the bench — to play.

And it ended in the most fitting of fashions. It ended with a come-from-behind victory in the bottom of the ninth inning. It ended as it started with Bill Plummer scoring from third base on an infield hit by Cesar Geronimo, just as the season's opening game had ended on George Foster's infield hit.

The regular season was history, The Big Red Machine having won 108 games, having outdistanced Los Angeles by twenty. The Machine had won sixty-four at home, more than any team in National League history. An astounding 2,315,603, a club record, paid to see The Big Red Machine play the major leagues' best baseball of 1975.

It had been a memorable season but it was only just beginning. The Reds had won nothing yet. They had made the playoffs before. They had made the World Series before. But they had not won a world's championship in thirty-five years.

"Until you get that ring that the commissioner buys, you haven't won anything," said Pete Rose.

PLAYOFF PIRACY

For a team that had won 108 games and had won its division by twenty games, The Big Red Machine was faced with more of a challenge from the Pittsburgh Pirates in the National League playoffs than one might have suspected. While the players were supremely confident in their ability to beat Pittsburgh and beat it easily, the populace of Cincinnati held no such feelings.

They fretted that the Pirates were going to pitch nothing but left-handed starters at their beloved Reds.

Seemingly unbeatable against right-handers, as an 82-32 record would indicate, the Reds had shown themselves to be mere mortals when a left-hander stepped on the mound, winning just 26 of 48 decisions from southpaws.

They fretted, too, about the scheduling of the playoffs. Five days existed between the end of the regular season and the opening of the playoffs, a situation that came about only so NBC-TV could have the opening playoff game on a Saturday. The Reds were notorious for playing poorly after a day off. What would they do after five days off, having ended the season with ten wins in their last eleven games? Would they cool off?

They fretted, too, about Pittsburgh having the home advantage in the playoffs. Scheduled to open in Cincinnati with two games, the playoffs then were to move to Three Rivers Stadium for three games if they were necessary. It was more than just a bit absurd that a team which won 108 games over the regular season received no benefit from it, instead actually finding itself at a disadvantage. Sparky Anderson called for the playoffs to be extended to seven games in the future to make a fairer test. He called for the team with the best record to have the advantage of playing the fifth game in its own home park, a move designed to help the Reds. Cincinnati after all was 64-17 at home and just 44-37 on foreign soil.

And then there was the jinx. The Reds were to open the playoffs at home and no team since the National League playoffs were instigated in 1969 had ever opened at home and won. All this was talked about as the days dragged slowly by. The only favorable thing about the playoffs, the citizens seemed to think, was that twice before the Reds and Pirates had tangled in playoffs and each time the Reds had walked off with the pennant. Jinx or not, Jimmy The Greek came out and made the Reds a 7-5 choice. At the local bookmakers' emporiums you couldn't get down on the Reds at less than 8-5.

As a surprise to no one, Sparky Anderson announced that Jack Billingham, his slumping right-hander, would not start against the Pirates in the playoffs. Little Fred Norman, instead, would have that honor in the second game.

Billingham, a strong, silent type, was hurt. He held it in, though, saying nothing stronger than "I'm down. My confidence is a little shot. Every athlete goes up and down but it seems I've been down a long time."

Almost mechanically the Reds were preparing themselves for Pittsburgh. Daily they digested the scouting report, studying strengths and weaknesses. They were certain they were the better team and wanted to take advantage of the areas in which their superiority was at its greatest. Those areas were on defense and with speed.

To the Cincinnati Reds speed meant one thing—Joe Morgan. He was the man in the middle, the man around whom the entire running game of the Reds revolved. He had already been named the best player in baseball in a computerized study, earning him a bonus of $10,000. He was the favorite for the Most Valuable Player award.

But Joe Morgan had history with which to contend. History said that Joe Morgan found the ice thin in the playoffs. In 1972 he was moving along beautifully until he jammed his heel stepping on first base. The result was an injury that slowed him and by World Series time he was merely a shadow of himself, hitting .125 against Oakland.

In 1973 it was total disaster, the New York Mets completely controlling him. He scored but one run, had but one hit and put together a .100 batting average. The Reds lost.

Joe Morgan knew he was expected to lead the Reds past Pittsburgh. He knew of the past failures but he didn't worry.

"I've failed before and been okay," he said. "I'll either do it or I'll fail. I can accept defeat for myself. I can accept it for myself much more than for the team. When it hurts is when you feel you let the guys down."

Joe Morgan's playoff preparations had begun more than a month earlier. The Reds still did not know whom they would be facing in the playoffs, Pittsburgh being involved in a race that included Philadelphia, St. Louis, and New York.

One afternoon Morgan and Sparky Anderson huddled in a corner of the clubhouse. Morgan had been batting third in the Cincinnati order almost all season. Now he had an idea.

He told Anderson that he figured Pittsburgh was going to win in the East, an observation with which Anderson totally agreed. Morgan said that if Pittsburgh won, chances were the Pirates would throw all left-handers at the Reds. Again Anderson agreed.

"If you'll bat me second I can put more pressure on Pittsburgh," Morgan said. Again Anderson concurred. Morgan batting second was more of a weapon on the bases than batting third. He would be freer to run and his running would have greater effect, probably coming with one or none out.

It was decided that Joe Morgan would move up into the Number 2 spot against Pittsburgh's left-handed pitching, outfielder Ken Griffey dropping to seventh in the order.

"Over a 162-game schedule it was better to have Morgan third," explained Anderson. "But for five games with everything so important Morgan can be a much greater factor hitting second."

The Reds were certain they could run on Pirate catcher Manny Sanguillen. They were certain also that the Pittsburgh pitchers—Jerry Reuss, Jim Rooker, and John Candelaria—had no chance of keeping the runners close.

So weak in fact was Sanguillen defensively that Pittsburgh manager Danny Murtaugh considered catching Duffy Dyer. In the end Sanguillen's .328 batting average won out over his defensive deficiencies. He would catch for the Pirates.

Morgan said he didn't care who the catcher was. "I don't steal off the catcher," he said. The Cincinnati game plan was designed to put as much pressure on the Pittsburgh defense as possible; a defense so lacking that even its own pitchers were critical of it.

As the season wound to a close Jim Rooker had had enough of it all. "I'm out there busting my butt and those clowns are dogging it," Rooker suggested. "This is the worst defense in baseball."

A day before the playoffs were to begin, Rooker still was being a witness for the prosecution of the defense, speaking out against his own teammates.

"How many championship clubs are not good defensive clubs?" he asked. "Which we aren't. This is a hitting organization. You come in, they give you a bat and it's hit, hit, hit. We make a lot of fundamental errors. You make a mistake once or twice, you should take stock. In time, you shouldn't be making the same mistakes. You'd think after playing a whole season together ... but we made all the same mistakes last year."

The Reds were going to run, to force mistakes. They were going to steal. It wasn't going to be instinctive base stealing either. Morgan was going to see to that.

During practice each day during the week, Morgan gathered The Red Rabbits around him — Dave Concepcion, Ken Griffey, George Foster. They ducked into the coaches' quarters where there was a videotape machine. And on the machine every day was the taped replay of the Pirate pitchers working with men on base. A scientist, Morgan knew in his own mind what each man did to give away his move. He wanted to share this knowledge with the others.

They started with Jerry Reuss, the talented left-hander who was to start the opening playoff game. Morgan stood by the screen as the others watched. He ran the machine, pointing out flaws. He would run it once, twice, a third time. He did it until they knew what to look for, how to spot it, when to go. "I'm not sure it helps them technically," Morgan said, "but it will help their confidence and that is the big thing."

Saturday, October 4, came around and, as winning pitcher Don Gullett was to say, "It wasn't 'Be Kind to Pirates Day.' "

The Reds, with Gullett pitching a complete game and driving in three runs with two hits, one of them his first professional home run, rushed to an 8-3 victory. But it wasn't Gullett, despite two standing ovations from the 54,633 who were crammed into Riverfront Stadium, who was the difference in this game.

It was Morgan. "Joe Morgan did more for us today than anyone else," marveled Anderson. "When we were down he opened the game for us." Joe Morgan did not get a hit in the game. It didn't matter.

The Reds, trailing 2-1 in the third inning, saw Morgan draw a leadoff walk. "I'm gonna steal second," he thought.

And steal second he did. "I'm gonna steal third," he now thought. And steal third he did.

Reuss was shaken. Sanguillen was destroyed. In three innings Morgan had stolen three bases. Before the third inning was over the Reds had scored three runs and Reuss was out of the game.

The groundwork had been laid. Little Joe Morgan was going to dominate the Pirates just as he had dominated Jerry Reuss. Reuss stood on the mound knowing Morgan was going to steal. He looked over and Morgan had a tremendous lead off first, nearly fourteen feet. He threw over. Nothing. Not even close. He could not intimidate the 5-foot-7 Morgan. "No one," Morgan says, "can dictate my lead. I dictate what lead I'll get."

Reuss tried some head fakes. Morgan wasn't watching his head. He had studied Jerry Reuss and knew just when to take off. Sanguillen had no chance. "No catcher could have thrown me out with the jumps I got," boasted Morgan. No one disagreed.

The tipoff on Sunday's second game of the playoffs probably came as the second inning concluded. Rooker had just thrown strike three past Pete Rose, Sanguillen grabbing the baseball for the out.

Normally, when a batter strikes out for the final out of an inning, the catcher will roll the ball toward the mound, sometimes playing a little game with himself to see just how close he can come to getting it up on the rubber.

Manny Sanguillen rolled the baseball to third base.

"He's trying to head the next Cincinnati runner off at third base," said a wit in the press box.

It was to be that kind of day for Sanguillen. The Reds attempted seven steals against him. They succeeded on every one. In two games The Red Rabbits had stolen ten straight bases. With the 6-1 triumph they now led the playoffs two games to none, needing only to win one of three games in Pittsburgh.

In this game, George Foster and Morgan each stole one base, Dave Concepcion stole two, and Ken Griffey stole three.

Sanguillen, a happy Panamanian, managed somehow to wear the perpetual smile that dominates his personality.

"What can you do?" he asked rhetorically. "We just have to forget what happened here and start over. You have to give Cincinnati credit. They steal every chance they get and that's what you have to do to win."

In reality, there was nothing Sanguillen or anyone else could do. Cincinnati's pitching, first Gullett, then Norman and Rawly Eastwick, had quieted Pittsburgh's fabled bats.

Defensively, the Reds had played immaculate baseball. And they had run and run and run. In the sixth inning of game Number 2 Griffey had opened with a single, stolen second and then third. After a walk to Cesar Geronimo, relief pitcher Kent Tekulve was so shaken, so unsure, that he balked, the Reds being given a run. The Reds were forcing mistakes.

"We're making it exciting with the steals," laughed Griffey. "Without 'em these games would have been dull."

The running of the Reds was so dominant that it went virtually unnoticed in the second game that Tony Perez hit a two-run homer in the first inning, enough to win the game, and added a couple of singles to finish with three runs batted in.

Monday was an off day. The Reds worked out in Three Rivers Stadium in Pittsburgh. They were less than thrilled with the day of rest, having everything going their way.

The locker room was abuzz after the workout, players

dressing to get back to the hotel, maybe play poker, maybe go to dinner. Most of them wanted to watch Monday Night Football. Johnny Bench walked into Sparky Anderson's office. He held aloft a pair of yellow casual shoes. "I'll be wearing 'em again tomorrow," said Bench. "You better be," answered Anderson.

Superstition is a big part of the game of baseball. The Cincinnati Reds, as good as they were, as confident as they were, still were looking for any edge they could get and Johnny Bench's casual shoes were just a little bit more of an edge. Bench had been given the shoes at a golf tournament in California over the winter.

"They were really comfortable," he explained. They were so comfortable that he wore them throughout spring training. He had the best spring of his life.

Once the regular season started, though, Johnny Bench filed the shoes away in a closet. The Reds of course got off on the wrong foot. Or at least had the right foot in the wrong shoe.

Coming home from the road at 20-20 Bench pulled the shoes out of the closet and wore them to the ball park. The Reds won. He wore them again and they won . . . and again . . . and again.

"Forty-one out of fifty," said Bench. He filed the shoes away in his closet saying, "we had it all won then." Now for the playoffs the lucky yellow shoes were out and the Reds were still winning.

"I don't believe in superstition but you can't argue with forty-one out of fifty," said Bench.

In another corner of the locker room waiting for the players to dress stood Mario Nunez. Everyone with the Reds knew Mario Nunez. They called him "The Cuban," he being of Cuban descent but never having seen Cuba. Nunez was born and raised in Ibor City, Florida, the Cuban district in Tampa. The Reds train in Tampa during the spring and Mario Nunez over the years became one of the many camp followers.

Whenever the Reds would play in Atlanta Nunez would show up, preparing a huge pot of black beans and rice, a delicacy the players would devour after a game.

By playoff time, though, Mario Nunez had become something more important than a supplier of beans and rice to the Reds. He had become their good luck charm.

It started opening day against the Dodgers. He was Pete Rose's house guest for the opening series, a Cincinnati sweep. He took in six games in Atlanta. The Reds won all six. Now, he had returned to Cincinnati for the playoffs. The Reds won two. Mario Nunez had seen Cincinnati play eleven times. Each time The Big Red Machine had won. There was no way Mario Nunez was going to be allowed to miss the third game in Pittsburgh.

"Sparky told me he would kiss my bald head if they win again," Mario Nunez revealed. He leaned forward showing off the bald spot. "They will win. They cannot lose when I am there."

As it worked out the Reds were going to need all the luck they could get in the third game of the 1975 playoffs. The Pirates in their stay-alive effort had selected John Candelaria, a 6-foot-7 inch rookie left-hander to go against Gary Nolan.

If Manny Sanguillen were to wind up the symbol of the Pittsburgh defeat, then John Candelaria, twenty-one, was to wind up the hero in defeat. Never before in the playoffs had anyone pitched so well, so overpoweringly.

But it wasn't enough to give Pittsburgh a reprieve.

John Candelaria struck out the first four Reds he faced. He struck out seven of the first nine. He struck out eleven of the first eighteen. After six innings, pumping fast ball after fast ball over the plate, then spicing it with a devastating curve, John Candelaria had stopped Cincinnati on one hit.

There were no stolen bases because only one Red reached base, he not stopping long enough at any base to attempt a steal. Dave Concepcion had hit a home run.

Gary Nolan, matching Candelaria all the way, protected the 1-0 lead Concepcion had given him until the sixth when Al Oliver clubbed a two-run homer. Pittsburgh led 2-1, and Candelaria was fully in charge.

The seventh inning drifted by. Then it was the eighth. Ken Griffey and Cesar Geronimo struck out. Candelaria now had fourteen strikeouts.

Merv Rettenmund was called on by Anderson to pinch-hit and he fought Candelaria for a walk. Now Pete Rose stepped in. Candelaria delivered and Rose took a mighty cut, the baseball flying over the left-field fence. The Reds now led 3-2, and Candelaria departed, all 46,355 fans on their feet to cheer their new-found hero.

The game went into the bottom of the ninth inning, Rawly Eastwick on in relief. Bases loaded, two out, Duffy Dyer at the plate. The Reds were one out from the National League title. Rawly Eastwick walked Dyer, forcing in the run that tied the game. The Pirates lived yet.

Ramon Hernandez, a crafty left-handed relief pitcher, was now on for Pittsburgh and Griffey, hitless all night, was the Cincinnati batter.

Even before the game had started Rose had preached to Griffey. "If you get a chance, bunt," Rose instructed, knowing Candelaria was a left-handed pitcher who could give Griffey problems.

Ken Griffey had not bunted. Now he was facing Hernandez. Curve for strike one. Curve for strike two. Nothing but curves, that's all Griffey was seeing.

"Well," thought Griffey, "he's going to throw me another curve. I might as well go ahead and try to lay it down. If I get it fair I have a chance for a hit."

Two strikes, no balls and Ken Griffey bunted. The Pirates were shocked. Rose was shocked. "I didn't expect him to bunt with two strikes," said the man who put the idea in Griffey's mind.

The ill-fated Sanguillen sprang from behind the plate. He fielded the ball and he threw to first. Griffey was safe. Eleven consecutive steals, now this. The threat of the steal was there again and Hernandez knew it. Ruffled by the happening and expectation of things to come, this thirty-six-year-old pitcher balked. Griffey was at second base.

Geronimo, pulling the ball on the ground to the right side, got Griffey to third. It was Eastwick's turn to hit but out of the dugout, instead, came Ed Armbrister.

Armbrister, a little-used reserve outfielder who grew up in the Bahamas playing baseball in a graveyard after making a field by turning over the crosses, now was being called on to win the pennant for the Reds.

During the regular season he had batted only sixty-five times and averaged just .185. His reputation was as a good defensive outfielder but twice he dropped routine fly balls, once costing the Reds a ball game. Now here he was just as he had been telling people he would be.

"I will do something to help win the playoffs," Ed Armbrister had predicted before the playoffs started. And do something he did, hitting a fly ball to deep center. Griffey came jogging home and the Reds were ahead by a run, the lead soon growing to 5-3 when Rose singled and scored on a double by Morgan.

Forgotten now was the brilliance of Candelaria. It was over for Pittsburgh and about to start again for Cincinnati. Pedro Borbon came on, retired three Pirates in the bottom

163

of the tenth inning, and for the third time in six years a flag flew over Cincinnati.

The Boston Red Sox were next.

SPYING ON THE RED SOX

Every time Ray Shore walks into Fenway Park the same pictures keep creeping into his mind. Long ago he stopped trying to keep them out. There was no way.

It was the same this time, early September, 1975. Ray Shore was about to begin scouting the Boston Red Sox for the Cincinnati Reds just in case Boston should somehow upend Oakland in the American League playoffs and represent the American League in the World Series. Things were pretty much the same. "The Green Monster" still dominated the ball park just as Ray Shore remembered it had.

Ray Shore had started his career as a catcher. A tall, barrel-chested man, he was the possessor of a strong throwing arm and a weak bat. World War II came along to interrupt Shore's budding career and he was assigned to the U.S. Army Air Corps, earned a commission and was eventually stationed in Algiers, North Africa. There he made a decision.

He would give up catching to take advantage of his arm. He would become a pitcher.

"I could always throw hard," Ray Shore now recalls. "Real hard. Pitching against guys who didn't have much experience during the time I was in the service I was very impressive." So impressive was Shore that he was tabbed "The Bob Feller of North Africa." He would strike out fifteen, maybe sixteen a game. And just to make him more effective he was wild.

When he left the service after the war was over he returned to the only thing he knew — baseball — joining the St. Louis Browns for spring training. It was 1946. Shore did not even bring a catcher's mitt with him. He was now a pitcher. When the Browns broke camp, Shore was assigned to Toledo. By the end of the season, though, the Browns had called him up to have a look. He pitched in only one game that year, working one inning, giving up three hits and a walk along with two runs.

It was 1948 before Shore returned to the big leagues, getting his only major league win. But Shore's memories of Fenway Park go back to 1949. It was hot, very hot, about one hundred degrees.

As usual, the Browns fell way behind, 8-2 in the

second inning. Zack Taylor was manager of the Browns and not wanting to use up his pitching staff in a game that was already lost he called on Shore to relieve, telling him it was his game the rest of the way. The situation was one that could make a pitcher's blood curdle, bases loaded, Ted Williams up. Ray Shore came on and with two strikes on Williams threw a change-up. Williams struck out.

"I didn't even have a change-up," said Shore. "It was no wonder I fooled him."

Ray Shore got out of that jam. He was to get out of few others. Later in the game he tried another change-up to Williams. This time it didn't fool him. He hit it halfway up the bleachers in right center for a home run. In all, Boston got sixteen runs off Ray Shore that day. He has no idea how many hits he gave up.

"So many balls hit the wall they had to repair it after the game," Shore now jokes. "And a few balls went over it." He recalls the ninth inning. As there always seemed to be, the bases were loaded, two were out. The heat had drained every ounce of strength Shore had. The score was 24-4.

Out to the mound walked Taylor. He took one look at his pitcher, his face flushed, his uniform drenched, already having allowed sixteen runs.

"You all right, kid?" he asked.

Ray Shore almost fainted on the spot. But he finished it off.

The next day was more of the same, Boston scoring more than twenty runs. And the following day the Browns finally won one, Ned Garver tricking the Red Sox to hold on for a 13-12 victory.

Is it any wonder that Ray Shore remembers it all when he walks into Fenway Park and somehow can't quite compare the team he is watching with the team he pitched against—Williams, Vern Stephens, Bobby Doerr, Dom DiMaggio, Johnny Pesky?

"The Red Sox today don't scare you like the old club did," he says. Of course, Shore doesn't have to pitch against today's Red Sox.

Ray Shore had been the advanced major league scout for the Reds since 1968. Dave Bristol, then manager of the Reds, was planning on dropping Shore from his coaching staff to bring in his own people. The Reds were going to make Shore their minor league pitching instructor but Bristol was a believer in advanced scouting. He asked that Shore be put in that position. Bob Howsam agreed.

"It was the greatest thing that ever happened to me," Shore now says.

An advanced major league scout serves a threefold purpose. He acts first as a scout, forwarding to the club the strengths and weaknesses of upcoming opponents, always being in the town ahead of the Reds. As a second duty he compares players, allowing the Reds to evaluate their own personnel better.

Finally, and perhaps most important, he rates the players on other teams and in the American League for evaluation when it comes time to make a trade. Shore's judgment in fact may be the most important consideration Bob Howsam uses when he goes after a player.

Now he was scouting the Red Sox just as he had scouted the Pittsburgh Pirates for the playoffs. His report on the Pirates was unerring. "Basically," he explained, "we knew the Pirates. So I tried to get detailed, a little finer on defense."

Ray Shore put together charts showing where the Pirates' tendencies were to hit the ball. It worked with precision, few baseballs getting into the gaps for extra base

Moments before the World Series of 1975 opened in Cincinnati, The Big Red Machine stands through the playing of "The Star-Spangled Banner."

—*Fred Straub, Cincinnati Enquirer Photo*

Ed Armbrister and Red
Sox catcher Carlton Fisk
collide at the plate in
third game of World
Series as umpire Larry
Barnett looks on, starting
fiery controversy. Barnett
ruled no interference on
Cincinnati hitter, bringing
Fisk and Boston manager
Darrell Johnson out to
argue.—*Wide World Photos—A*
—Fred Straub, Cincinnati
Enquirer Photo—B

B

Johnny Bench connects for a home run in the fourth inning of the third game of the World Series to wipe out a Boston lead and start a Big Red Machine barrage that buried the Red Sox.—*Bob Lynn, Cincinnati Enquirer Photo*

Boston catcher Carlton Fisk ends the sixth game of the World Series, considered one of the best games ever played, with a dramatic home run in the 12th inning off Pat Darcy.—*Bob Lynn, Cincinnati Enquirer Photo*

Bill Lee threw one too many blooper pitches to Tony Perez in the seventh game of the World Series, this one being driven far over the left field screen as Carlton Fisk, the Boston catcher, waits in vain. Umpire is Art Frantz. The homer cut Boston's lead to 3-2.
—*Wide World Photos*

Joe Morgan bloops the hit to centerfield that brought The Big Red Machine the 1975 World Championship. The single drove in Ken Griffey with the winning run of the seventh game and came off Boston pitcher Jim Burton.
—*Wide World Photos*

The two most valuable Reds, Joe Morgan (l) and Pete Rose celebrate after The Big Red Machine clinched the Western Division championship. It was the earliest clinching in National League history, coming on September 7.—*Wide World Photos*

Pat Darcy (l) and Rawly Eastwick, two of the young pitchers who helped carry The Big Red Machine, whoop it up in the locker room after the Reds beat Boston in the seventh game of the 1975 World Series.—*Wide World Photos*

Fountain Square in downtown Cincinnati is jammed to the limits by thousands of fans who turned out to welcome home the world champion Reds after beating Boston in the World Series.

—*Dick Swaim, Cincinnati Enquirer Photo*

Reds' catcher John Bench salutes the women watching the "welcome home" champions parade through a store window with the "We're No. 1" sign after winning the world championship.
—*Ed Reinke, Cincinnati Enquirer Photo*

Tony Perez, a big cigar clenched between his teeth, rides before the thousands of fans in Cincinnati who turned out for a parade to welcome home the world champions. His wife, Petucka, and son, Victor, are in the back seat.—*Wide World Photos*

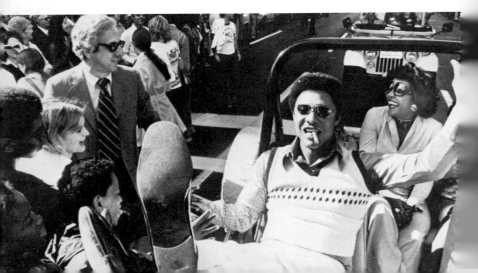

hits. This was his goal. A team without a great deal of speed, the Pirates were almost helpless without being able to get extra base hits. They fell in three games. Ray Shore also had pointed out that Manny Sanguillen had no chance of throwing out a Cincinnati base stealer. Running at will the Reds stole eleven straight bases on Sanguillen.

The Red Sox presented a slightly different problem than Pittsburgh. To begin with, Carlton Fisk had a reputation as one of the best catchers in the game. Ray Shore watched Carlton Fisk and had his own ideas.

"Fisk showed an above average arm in infield practice," explained Shore. "On certain plays he threw exceptionally well. But he isn't too quick releasing the ball and he's not accurate. He's better than Sanguillen. With Sanguillen it was cut and dried. Sanguillen needed his pitcher to hold the runner close, a perfect pitch to handle and then he still had troubles."

Ray Shore reported that Fisk could be run on. He also said that it wouldn't be as easy as with Pittsburgh, the Boston pitchers—especially Luis Tiant—being better than the Pirates at holding a runner close.

So what happened? The first two Reds in the World Series to try and steal—Morgan and Foster—were thrown out.

"I was not second-guessing myself. I didn't change my opinion. I wasn't concerned. I figured we'd keep running until Fisk buried us," said Shore. Fisk never threw another runner out as the Reds swiped the last nine bases they attempted.

Ray Shore's report contained another observation. The Boston Red Sox were a fast ball-hitting team. This was an observation that Sparky Anderson just couldn't accept. "I'd always heard the American League was a breaking ball league. The Red Sox hit .275 as a team. You can't hit that high if you can't hit breaking balls," said Anderson.

In the first game Don Gullett, a fastball pitcher, worked for the Reds. The Reds lost. In the second game Jack Billingham worked for the Reds. Using his curve ball Billingham eased past Boston.

"Jack Billingham showed us something today," Sparky Anderson said after the game. "He proved something to us that we had to have proved. I can't tell you what it was but as the World Series progresses you'll see it."

Most people read into Anderson's statement. Instead of thinking about Shore's scouting report they thought that Billingham had proved himself capable of pitching again, something he hadn't done for half of the year. Anderson, however, does not speak symbolically. He simply meant that Billingham had proven that breaking balls were the proper way to pitch the Red Sox.

Take Carlton Fisk. Shore's report read that Fisk liked the fast ball low and from the middle of the plate on in. "Every ball he hit after the second game came on a fast ball in that zone. His home run in Cincinnati, his foul home run in Cincinnati, and the home run that won the sixth game in Boston."

There was one other factor Shore took into account as he scouted the Red Sox. It was "The Green Monster" in left field. "The wall was always on my mind," Shore explained. "I was especially afraid of the left-handers with power — Bernie Carbo, Yaz, Fred Lynn. Those guys, swinging late, could cause real trouble.

"I kept thinking what a difference Catfish Hunter would have made to Oakland in the playoffs. He would have won twice. He throws the good breaking ball and has that pinpoint control. The Red Sox would not have been able to beat him."

Shore, while always aware of The Green Monster, tried to play it down when reporting to his players. "I didn't want to overemphasize it," said Shore. "I talked to Bench about it."

The typical conversation went like this: "John, I know you can get into Dwight Evans by throwing the ball inside, but if the game's on the line you can't afford to try it," Shore would say.

Bench would agree. In Fenway Park for the most part Cincinnati pitchers tried to keep the ball away from right-handed hitters. It worked. Ray Shore's entire scouting report worked. It could be seen throughout the series.

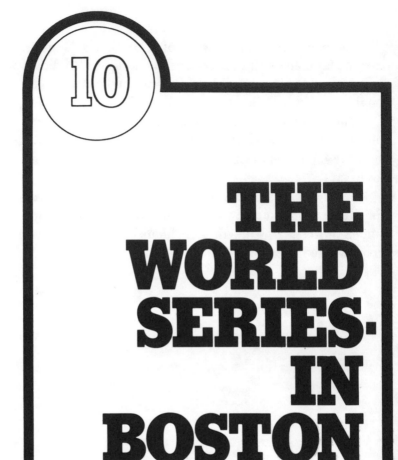

10

THE WORLD SERIES- IN BOSTON

Fountain Square in the heart of downtown Cincinnati was jammed, a pleasant sun sitting in a clear blue sky above, spraying a certain kind of happy radiation upon the 12,000 who gathered to welcome home their heroes.

The Big Red Machine had returned from Boston as champions of the world. Bowie Kuhn stepped up to a microphone and was cheered, conservative old Cincinnati perhaps being the only city in the country that will always cheer the commissioner of baseball.

"I came to bring you something," echoed the voice of Kuhn off the tall downtown buildings. "I came to bring you something this city deserves and this great team deserves. I bring you the championship of the world trophy."

Cincinnati said thank you with a loud roar.

It had started so long ago, two weeks before the masses gathered at the fountain. The World Series, Cincinnati against Boston, the most exciting World Series anyone could remember.

It had started with the Reds a heavy favorite to beat the Boston Red Sox, the American League champion, a team that combined youth and experience and that was owned by lovable Tom Yawkey.

It had started with a psychological ploy on the part of the Reds. Cincinnati was a running team, a team that based its very existence on its ability to steal bases and force mistakes on the part of the opposition. Stealing bases on the Boston Red Sox, though, was no easy chore, multiplied many times in degree of difficulty when Luis Tiant was on the mound, as he was scheduled to be in the opener in Boston.

Tiant was the owner of a most unorthodox pitching style. With no one on base he was a whirling dervish seemingly turning his back in defiance upon the hitter. With runners on base he did some strange things. As he came to his set position his arms would come down in a herky-jerky, stop-and-go motion. It seemed he never was set.

Then, in throwing to first base, his move sometimes bordered on a balk. Still, Luis Tiant had never been called for a balk. Running on Luis Tiant was indeed going to be a challenge for The Red Rabbits.

While waiting for the long days between the playoffs

173

and the World Series to pass, word filtered out of Boston that Sparky Anderson had put his hands upon some film of Tiant pitching from a stretch and had forwarded that film to baseball officials to study.

"Absolutely untrue," shouted Anderson. "A total lie," he said. "Any more stories like that and I'm closing my doors to reporters," he said. He had forwarded no film to baseball officials, he said. The story, though, had to come from somewhere. A plant? Perhaps. The source of the story never was pinned down.

"All I want," said Anderson, "is a clarification of the balk rule from the umpires in our preseries meeting. I want it thoroughly discussed and I want it decided what is a balk and what isn't. I have nothing against Luis Tiant. But I say if he isn't balking then let's forget about balks. You might as well throw the rule book out."

Masterfully, Sparky Anderson had planted the seed. He had Tiant thinking. He had the umpires thinking. He had the public thinking. Whether or not Luis Tiant balked became almost as important a question as who won the opener.

And Anderson's smoke screen served as cover for another important aspect of the 1975 World Series. The manager of the Cincinnati Reds had decided that his second-game pitcher would be Jack Billingham, the pitcher who had slumped so badly and pitched so ineffectively over the last six weeks of the season.

Billingham would work game Number 2 while Fred Norman, the miniature left-hander who had pitched so brilliantly through the second half of the season and who had turned in such an outstanding performance against Pittsburgh in the playoffs, was shuffled off to the bull pen.

With the furor over the Tiant balk controversy at its

highest pitch, little was made of the pitching change. But Fred Norman made note of it. "I'm upset," he snapped to reporters just two days before the opening of the series. "I believe I should be pitching. I believe I'm one of the guys who got us here."

Anderson's thinking was that Billingham, being a sinkerball pitcher, would be more effective in Boston's Fenway Park with The Green Monster looming down the left field line, and that Anderson would need a second left-hander in the bull pen to go with Will McEnaney in a seven-game series.

Fred Norman was not the only member of the World Series cast who was upset as play was about to begin. There was also Carlton Fisk, the Boston catcher. Fisk was considered the best catcher in the American League. However, he was faced with comparisons of himself with Johnny Bench, who was considered the best catcher in baseball, if not the best catcher ever.

"Comparisons of one player to another are unfair," said Fisk. "It is not me against Bench. It is the Red Sox against the Reds."

Fisk, however, was also to add a prophetic statement. "Me against Bench? I almost have to come out the bum don't I? They run an awful lot," said Fisk.

The two cities were starved for victory. Boston had not won a World Series since 1918. The Reds had not won since 1940. Even the governors got into the act. Massachusetts governor Michael Dukakis started it all by offering to bet twenty pounds of Massachusetts codfish against a bushel of Ohio corn that the Red Sox would win. Ohio governor James Rhodes turned him down, saying privately, "I don't want to take the guy's fish." But when Dukakis notified the press of his offer Rhodes said, "If Dukakis is determined to give

175

that much fish away, I'll match the cod with ten pounds of Lake Erie perch and ten pounds of Ohio River catfish. I guess we can't expect a subway rider from Massachusetts to know we harvest sweet corn in the summer, not in October."

It was almost time for the World Series. Friday, October 10th, the Cincinnati Reds got their first look at Boston's Fenway Park with The Green Monster in left field. Johnny Bench looked at the wall and said, "I thought it would be taller."

And sounding disappointed, he added, "and closer."

Johnny Bench stepped into the batting cage and lined three home runs over the screen. Brooks Lawrence, a retired pitcher, was throwing batting practice. Time after time Bench rocketed baseballs into the screen above The Green Monster.

"Forget about the wall, Brooks," hollered Bench to the batting practice pitcher and everyone laughed, knowing the Cincinnati pitchers had been instructed to "forget about the wall."

As the Reds held batting practice George Foster was stationed in left field taking ball after ball off The Green Monster, trying to learn its strange bounces, its many intricacies. The Cincinnati plan was to converge on the wall. On balls hit to left field Foster was to go back to the wall. Shortstop Dave Concepcion was to sprint into the outfield should the ricochet bounce away from Foster. And center-fielder Cesar Geronimo was to come over to take away weird caroms.

"It is," said Sparky Anderson, "the only way you can handle the wall. You must surround it." As it turned out despite all the worry and preparation the wall did not play a very big part in this World Series.

As it always is with the Series, there was a tremendous preseries buildup. Everyone had his own opinion. Perhaps the most prophetic was a scouting report published in the Cincinnati *Enquirer*. Within that scouting report was one sentence that was, in the long run, to capsulize the World Series.

"It is almost incomprehensible that a team with Denny Doyle, let go by Philadelphia and California, could win a pennant let alone a World Series," read the Cincinnati *Enquirer* story. That had to be the most meaningful thing written among the millions of words that came out before the World Series.

The 1975 World Series opened on Saturday, October 11, a dark and dreary day in Boston. But it was not dark and dreary for the Red Sox. They were to go one up in the series, Luis Tiant masterfully subduing Cincinnati's Big Red Machine on five hits as he outdueled Don Gullett.

Through the early going it was even, Tiant and Gullett retiring batter after batter. In the fourth inning for just one brief instant it appeared as if Anderson's psychological ploy was about to work.

One was out when Joe Morgan singled. There were 35,205 fans in the stands, most of them rooting for the Red Sox. Morgan took his lead off first. Tiant whirled and fired over. Before the ball had reached first base Nick Colosi, the first base umpire and working his first World Series game, had his hands up in the air and was shouting "balk."

"I saw a balk and I called it. What's the big deal about?" Colosi asked in the umpire's dressing room when it was all over, as if he didn't know about the Anderson-Tiant feud.

Tiant rushed first base steaming mad. "I knew they

were going to look for the balk," the thirty-four-year-old right-hander said. "That is unfair. I am mad that they called it." The call had disturbed Tiant. He was shouting in Spanish at Colosi. Tiant's mind was not on the game now, only on the balk call. Cecil Cooper, the Boston first baseman, collared Tiant and ushered him back toward the pitcher's mound.

"I realized while I was arguing that this is just what Cincinnati wants me to do. I just told myself not to get mad and to get back to thinking about pitching," said Tiant. And think about pitching he did. As the game progressed it became obvious that it wasn't Cincinnati's day. Time after time they hit the ball hard off Tiant. Time after time the Boston fielders were in the right place.

"This can't go on," shouted Pete Rose. But go on it did. In the first inning Morgan lined out. In the second inning Perez and Foster lined out. In the third inning Denny Doyle made a spectacular play on Ken Griffey. In the sixth inning Rose lined out. In the eighth inning Rose lined out.

Rose went hitless, ending a seventeen-game hitting streak he had carried through the final days of the season and the playoffs. "I would not mind hitting against Luis Tiant every day," said Rose. "I might go 0-for-100, but I wouldn't mind hitting against him."

Through six hard innings the game was scoreless. Then came the seventh. Luis Tiant was the leadoff hitter. He had batted once since 1972, the American League having adopted the designated hitter rule. In two years he had not batted at all.

Gullett got two quick strikes on him with fast balls. It was time for a mistake and Gullett made it, throwing a fork ball, an off-speed pitch, and Tiant slashed it to left field for a hit.

Dwight Evans now was the hitter and he was called on

to bunt. He laid down a good one, but Gullett pounced off the mound as only he can.

"Second base," shouted Johnny Bench.

Gullett, following instructions, wheeled and started to throw toward second. Just as he cocked his arm, his feet slipped on the wet grass. "I had nothing on the throw. It was on line. It just had no mustard," said Gullett.

Tiant who is less than the swiftest of runners was safe. Now the bottom was about to fall out on the Cincinnati Reds. Denny Doyle singled. Carl Yastrzemski singled. Gullett exited.

Bases loaded, one run in, Clay Carroll came jogging out of the bull pen. He pitched to one batter, Carlton Fisk, and walked him, forcing in a run. Captain Hook was back to the mound. He had seen enough of Carroll, calling in Will McEnaney.

McEnaney struck out Fred Lynn, then gave up singles to Rico Petrocelli and Rick Burleson. A sacrifice fly by Cecil Cooper gave Boston six runs. The first game of the series belonged to the Red Sox. The Big Red Machine was down 0-1 and Jack Billingham was going against Bill Lee in the second game.

As Sunday dawned it was obvious the weather was fit more for whaling than for baseball. It was cold, windy, and a light drizzle was falling. Had it been a regular season game they never would have played, but this was the World Series and NBC had to have a show.

It was Bill Lee who summed things up after the game as concisely as they could be summed up.

"What's your impression of the series so far?" Lee was asked.

"Tied," he answered.

The Reds had come from behind with two ninth-inning runs to win 3-2. Billingham had pitched brilliantly for the Reds. He pitched so well that Sparky Anderson commented that "Billingham taught us some things we thought were right and now we're assured of it." Anderson refused to go any farther.

As the ninth inning started, The Big Red Machine was looking at the wrong end of a 2-1 score. The Machine had been embarrassed, scoring one run in seventeen innings in "The Walled City." Now Johnny Bench was at the plate, leading off the ninth inning. His mind was working overtime. "I realized something had to happen. I even thought of bunting," he explained.

As he walked to the plate he looked at the Boston defense. They had overshifted on him, Denny Doyle moving to the left of second base.

"I know hitting to right field was what they wanted me to do. But they weren't giving me any pitches to pull at the wall. I figured I had to take a shot at it," said Bench.

Bill Lee let fly a fast ball. He described it as "two inches outside and an inch below the knee." Bench described the pitch as "up" but added, "the way I'm hitting I can't have any real idea where the pitch was." He lashed the ball into right field and wound up at second base.

As he reached second base Denny Doyle approached him. "Why don't you hit the ball where you're supposed to?" asked Doyle. Bench just shrugged his shoulders and smiled. Moments later the smile was to turn to laughter.

With two out and Dick Drago now on in relief Bench found himself at third base. Dave Concepcion was the hitter. One day earlier on Saturday, Concepcion had made the final out of the game against Luis Tiant.

As Concepcion walked to the plate to face Drago he thought to himself, "No way I will make the last out this time." He didn't. He hit a bouncer through the middle that Doyle backhanded behind second. He could not make a play. Bench came home and the game was tied.

Concepcion now stood at first looking toward Alex Grammas, the third base coach. The steal sign was flashed. It was a daring play especially since the Reds had not yet stolen a base against Fisk. The Red Sox catcher had nailed Joe Morgan earlier in the game. A day before he had thrown out George Foster.

Still, the Reds were confident they could run on Fisk and they succeeded as Concepcion stole second on a close play, oversliding the base and having to reach back with his hand.

"If he tags me a second time I'm out," said Concepcion. There was no second tag.

Now Ken Griffey stepped to the plate and he was to be the hero, slashing a double to left center that drove Concepcion home with the run that was to give the Reds their forty-eighth come-from-behind win, twenty-five of them in their final at bat.

The World Series was even, one game apiece, even though Cincinnati had not played its finest baseball. The time had come for the World Series to move to Cincinnati to Riverfront Stadium.

11

THE WORLD SERIES-IN CINCIN-NATI

When the Boston Red Sox arrived in Cincinnati they were in for a rude awakening. Their hotel was in suburban Sharonville, a full thirteen miles from Riverfront Stadium. They weren't happy about it. Downtown Cincinnati was completely booked up.

The National Rehabilitation Association was holding its fiftieth annual meeting in Cincinnati. The convention had been booked for five years. They had tied up 2,000 hotel rooms. Add to that the 1,000 members of the

American Racing Pigeon Union and you have the town completely sold out for the week of the World Series.

As tough as it was on the Red Sox it wasn't nearly as bad as it had been on the Reds when they arrived in Boston.

Unable to get enough rooms to accommodate the 155 members of the traveling party, the Reds had to split between two hotels. The players and their wives were to be quartered at the Statler-Hilton and the Statler-Hilton was not ready for them.

"My room," said pitcher Clay Kirby, "is so small I have to go outside to change my mind."

Two reporters were given a single room with one bed to share, something they remedied in a hurry. Ted Kluszewski, 250 pounds of muscle, received a room without a double bed. No fewer than ten of the players were in the lobby moments after checking in to complain about their rooms.

"I'll go anywhere. Just get me out of here," said Don Gullett, who almost never complains about anything.

In game Number 1 against Tiant, a right-hander, Joe Morgan had hit second. Sparky Anderson had wanted to go back to his old lineup, the one with Griffey hitting second and Morgan third, but had decided not to. With Morgan batting second the Reds swept the Pirates in the playoffs.

"I'm not a superstitious person," said Anderson. "But we'd won three in a row. Superstition got me." He stuck with the lineup that had won against Pittsburgh and he lost to Tiant. After that game he and his coaches huddled in his suite at the Statler-Hilton. "I want to go back to the old lineup when we go against Rick Wise," he told the coaches. "But I'm not going to do it until I talk to Morgan."

It seems absurd, doesn't it, a manager checking with a

player before making a change in the lineup? Not in the mind of Sparky Anderson.

"That's a big part of managing," said Anderson. "If a player accepts something that you want to do he'll be able to handle it a lot better than if he doesn't accept it."

At Fenway Park on Sunday, as the rain fell and the cold ate into one's flesh, Anderson approached Morgan. They walked into the trainer's room, Morgan's arm around Anderson. Anderson eased into his request.

"Hey, they got a right-hander going in the next game," said Anderson.

"I hope you want to say that you're going back to the old lineup," said Morgan.

"Well, I was going to say that," answered a surprised Anderson.

"Skip, we're on the same wave length," said Morgan.

The reason for the change was, against a right-hander like Rick Wise, Griffey and Morgan gave the Reds what Anderson described as "complete speed at the top of the lineup." Morgan had a bit different explanation for the switch.

"I want to hit third against right-handers because it gives us another RBI man and takes a little of the pressure off Tony and John and it gives me a chance to drive in some runs." So it was set. The Reds facing Rick Wise in game Number 3 would move Morgan into the Number 3 spot in the lineup.

Riverfront Stadium presented a new challenge to the Red Sox. In Boston on a grass field the outfielders had played ridiculously shallow, so shallow that the Reds dared them to try it when they got to the AstroTurf covered outfield in Cincinnati.

"You'd better have speed to play here," challenged Anderson.

Darrell Johnson, the Boston manager, accepted the challenge.

"If it tests our speed it will also test the Reds' speed," he said. "A good player can play in a brickyard. It doesn't matter what the surface is."

There were Red Sox who were familiar with Riverfront Stadium. Wise had pitched a no-hitter there in 1971 when he was working for the Philadelphia Phillies. To rub salt into the Reds' wounds that day he contributed two home runs. Two years later he pitched a one-hitter in Riverfront Stadium, Joe Morgan's ninth-inning hit ruining his bid for a second no-hitter.

And there was Carl Yastrzemski whose memories went back to 1970, to the All-Star that ended so smashingly with Pete Rose exploding into Ray Fosse at home plate in the twelfth inning to win the game for the National League. Despite his heroics Rose was not the most valuable player in the game. The honor belonged to Yaz, who collected four hits in six tries.

Yaz remembered Riverfront well. He remembered the trophy that came with the honor and what he did with it, presenting it to one Richard M. Nixon, then President of the United States, with the promise that Nixon would appear at the Boston baseball writers' banquet that winter.

Nixon didn't show.

Game Number 3 was to end in a swirl of controversy, the Boston Red Sox shouting foul. Morgan's bases-loaded single, with one out in the tenth inning, carried The Big Red Machine to a 6-5 victory and a two games to one lead in the World Series.

The controversy centered around Ed Armbrister and Carlton Fisk on a bunt play where the two collided. The stage was set like this.

Boston, on Dwight Evans' dramatic ninth-inning home run — the sixth homer of the game — had battled back from a 5-1 deficit to tie the game 5-5, forcing extra innings.

Facing Jim Willoughby who was to be the loser, Cesar Geronimo singled to lead off the tenth inning. Now Armbrister was called on to bat for winning pitcher Rawly Eastwick. Armbrister's orders were to bunt, which he did. The ball went straight down into the ground, then came straight up.

Fisk pounced from behind the plate and as he grabbed the ball he collided with Armbrister. Forcing his throw to second base he was off line and the ball sailed into centerfield. By the time Boston could retrieve the baseball Reds were at second and third.

"It was obvious interference because I had to push him out of the way," said Fisk. "When I pushed him out of the way he stopped. I probably tagged him . . . I don't know. It's just a shame to lose a World Series game on a lousy call like that."

"Of course he interfered with me," Fisk continued. "He stood right under the ball. It reminded me of a football game. You might as well just throw a cross-body block on the catcher and run to first base."

Larry Barnett, appearing in his first World Series and an American League umpire, would not rule interference despite a lengthy argument from Fisk and manager Darrell Johnson.

"I got no satisfaction," said Johnson of the argument. "I know my interpretation was that the man was out. The man running cannot come in contact with the man who is fielding the ball."

186

Barnett saw it differently. "I ruled it was simply a collision," said Barnett. "It is interference only when the batter intentionally gets in way of the fielder. Each man has an equal right."

The Red Sox could not accept that version of the play.

"Let us decide who wins and loses, not the umpires," shouted Dick Drago in the Boston locker room.

"It's a shame the game can't be decided by the players," said Wise, who allowed but four hits, three of them home runs and one a triple, before leaving.

"That evens the series 1-1-1. One for us, one for the Reds, one for the umpires," shouted another player.

The Reds, of course, saw the play differently.

"As I broke for first base he hit me in the back and reached over my head for the ball before I could continue on to first base," said Armbrister. "I stood there because he hit me in the back and I couldn't move." Reds' manager Sparky Anderson added that in his judgment there was no interference. "Any time you hit a ball you're entitled to run."

The decision stood, even though Barnett had erred in his explanation of why no interference had occurred. He had used the word "intentionally," a word that doesn't appear in the applicable rules. All Larry Barnett had to say was "I ruled there was no interference." It was a judgment call which could not be protested and the Red Sox were not to get back the game, a game that was won when Morgan, given the chance as the Number 3 hitter, singled to score Geronimo.

The following day the controversy continued. Armbrister had watched the television replay and had come to the conclusion that "I did not interfere."

Darrell Johnson, though, was of the opposite opinion. He remembered going out to argue with Barnett but he couldn't remember what was said. "Barnett stuttered a lot.

The words are now lost. I knew I was beating my head against a stone wall."

Darrell Johnson was asked about the collision. "Collision? I was thinking about collusion," he answered with a wry smile, collusion being defined in the dictionary as "a secret agreement between two or more persons to defraud a person of his rights often by forms of law."

Another question was fired at Johnson. "Barnett said he didn't think . . . "

Johnson interrupted. "He should have stopped right there," said Johnson.

Sparky Anderson merely said the controversy was blown all out of proportion. "It's over and the issue is closed," said the manager of the Cincinnati Reds.

The Reds led, two games to one, and now they had to face Luis Tiant again. The Reds were thinking now of ending it in five games, a thought that soon was to be erased as Tiant went all the way for the second time to win 5-4. The series again was tied 2-2, with the fifth game coming up.

This was the big game. The game the Reds had to win. A loss here and they were almost certain of losing the World Series. That the Reds were tied at all was something of a surprise because they had won two games without getting any kind of offensive help from Tony Perez, the man they look to for the big run batted in.

Tony Perez had been to the plate fourteen times and owned no hits. They were thinking now of Gil Hodges, who in 1952 had gone hitless twenty-one consecutive times in a World Series. The record for frustration belonged to Dal Maxvill, who managed somehow to go 0-for-22, but the standard was Hodges' 0-for-21, Hodges being a superior hitter.

As Tony Perez took his batting practice that night he explained, "I'm trying everything I can think of." He had watched videotapes of himself. He tried hitting a baseball off a tee. He had taken extra batting practice. "I can't stay back," Tony Perez explained. "I can't stay back on Tiant's fast ball and he is getting me out on breaking balls. He's got me up on my toes."

It had been an interesting battle in the series, Perez against Tiant. Both are Cuban. Both are class people.

"When Luis got on first base he called me 'Ugly,'" Perez recalled. "It is like you say 'Hello.'"

Both Perez and Tiant had shared the lonely experience of leaving their families behind in Cuba to come to the United States to play baseball. Toward the end of the 1975 season Luis Tiant's father, Luis Sr., was allowed to leave Cuba and see his son pitch in the major leagues. When that happened Perez sent Tiant a telegram telling him he was glad for him. "I know my father never see me play," said Perez. "My father he is very sick."

Still, Tony Perez was happy for Luis Tiant.

Now Perez was 0-for-14 and was saying, "I'm not pressing, I'm just in a slump. I'm too old to be pressing." Tony Perez had gone through it before. In his first World Series he had gone 1-for-18. In his next World Series he had hit .435. Through both series he remained the same person. Now you couldn't tell which way Tony Perez was going.

"I don't get mad easy but I feel bad," he admitted.

The fifth game opened and the Red Sox scored a first-inning run. In the second inning Tony Perez struck out, making him 0-for-15. It was to be the final frustration of the night for Perez. The rest of the night he was king.

In the fourth inning he tied the game with a home run off Reggie Cleveland. Then, in the sixth with the Reds winning 2-1, he came to the plate with two men on. He hit another home run. For the first time since 1959 a National League player had hit two home runs in a World Series

189

game. Tony Perez had given the Reds all the runs they needed.

They won 6-2 behind Don Gullett, who carried a two-hitter into the ninth inning before tiring and giving way to Rawly Eastwick.

"Don Gullett," said Darrell Johnson; "dominated the game. He was the Number one reason we got beat tonight."

But it was Perez' homers that were to be the real story. That and a misplay by the ill-fated Denny Doyle.

In the sixth inning the Reds led just 2-1 with no one out and Morgan on first base. Johnny Bench hit a perfect double-play ball to Doyle. Doyle, however, broke to his right and could not recover in time to make the play. The ball went as a single.

"I thought it was a sure double-play ball," said Bench.

"I reacted to what I saw. Then I didn't see anything. I lost the ball in Bench's uniform," said Doyle.

Perez, given the chance, unloaded his second home run and the game was over. The Reds were going to Boston leading in the series three games to two. They had only to split the remaining two games in Boston.

12

THE WORLD SERIES- RETURN TO BOSTON

As Joe Morgan spoke it was easy to tell he was the proprietor of a liquor store in Oakland, California. "We've got the champagne riding with us," he said. And ride it did, all the way back to Boston where the Cincinnati Reds had some good news and some bad news awaiting them.

The good news was that the players had been moved out of the Statler-Hilton and into Howard Johnson's. The bad news was that it was raining.

"It will rain for forty days and forty nights," predicted

Bill Lee, the Boston left-hander who was scheduled to pitch the sixth game of the series. He was almost right. It rained all day Friday. It rained Saturday. By nine-twenty a.m. Saturday, the sixth game of the World Series had been canceled.

"It's just a stay of execution for Boston," boasted Morgan.

"It doesn't matter if it rains today, tomorrow, Monday. We've still got to beat them two straight—sometime," said Carl Yastrzemski. Sunday came. More rain. Again, early in the morning the series was washed out. By now everyone was going crazy.

Terry Crowley, the Reds' Number 1 pinch hitter, had been writing a special column for *The Staten Island Advertiser*, his hometown newspaper. "They told me I didn't have to write a column and I was really glad. I was running out of things to say," he said as the Reds held an indoor workout at Tufts University.

He had learned the work of the newspaperman was not so easy. Carl Yastrzemski, writing for the Boston *Herald-American*, had learned the same thing. He was given the day off too.

There was, however, plenty to write about. Jack Billingham was mad. With the two days of rain Sparky Anderson had decided that he would bypass Billingham and pitch Gary Nolan in the sixth game with his ace Don Gullett, now rested and ready for the seventh game.

At the same time Bill Lee was mad. Darrell Johnson had decided that Tiant now had enough rest to pitch in the sixth game, Lee being held back for the seventh. For the record, Anderson reasoned that he went to Nolan rather than Billingham because Nolan could not pitch in relief.

"That explanation is not satisfactory to me," said Billingham.

The fact of the matter was that Anderson really felt Nolan's breaking ball would be more effective against Boston than Billingham's sinker. On Sunday, Anderson called both Billingham and Nolan into his office. He explained his decision to the two men, Billingham getting madder and madder as the manager spoke.

"Then," Billingham reported, "he said something that was supposed to make me smile, to ease the pain a little. I didn't appreciate it at all."

Anderson didn't expect Billingham to smile. "If he had I would have figured he didn't want to pitch in the game," Sparky Anderson said.

Jack Billingham, accused throughout his career of being laconic, no longer seemed so. "I'm supposed to be the guy who can keep the ball on the ground in Fenway Park," said Billingham. "I don't know why that should change now. This is a great disappointment to me since I pitched so well in here before.

"They pitched me because of 'The Green Monster' in left and we won. I'm disappointed and angry. I finally get my stuff together, pitch a good game, and they hit me in the side of the head with something like this.

"It seems like I just get stepped on a lot. They seem to think 'Good ol' Jack, he won't get mad. We'll push him around.' Well, I'm tired of being pushed around."

The Reds were edgy. They had lived in a hotel for three days and still had not played a game. They were going out of their minds.

Jolene Billingham, Jack's wife, probably felt it worst of all. "It's frustrating," she said. "We were both very disappointed in Sparky's decision. We found it difficult to accept because we couldn't quite understand why the change was made."

And still it rained. "I'm tired of the rain and I'm tired of washing clothes," Jolene Billingham continued. "I've been washing our clothes and hanging them out over the heater."

The Reds wanted to get it over with. Boston wanted to get on with it. The weather had taken its toll on the Red Sox. Owner Tom Yawkey was sick with the flu. Tiant had the flu. Dwight Evans had the flu.

"You have to play sick," said Evans. "You can't call in and tell them you're taking the day off. This is what you get paid for. It's part of the job."

The rainouts, had they helped anyone? Boston now had a well-rested Tiant, but the Reds had Gullett who was not going to be able to pitch at all, to pitch the seventh game.

"If Gullett isn't better than Bill Lee then I'm a maniac," said Anderson. The statement put the Cincinnati manager far out on a limb, but he was hoping Don Gullett would not have to pitch any more. He was hoping to win it in six games and he came so close.

Monday it rained again. The game was off. Bill Lee may have been right. It looked like rain for forty days and forty nights. Sparky Anderson thought about his pitching decision.

"I'm not sure I want to pitch Nolan with eight days rest," he confided. Ten minutes later, though, he was saying Nolan would pitch, explaining, "I can't have two of my guys mad at me."

Monday night most of the Reds watched the New York Giants upset O.J. Simpson and the Buffalo Bills. A bad omen? They thought not.

The Reds weren't the only ones who were going insane. It came out Monday night that the life of umpire Larry Barnett and his family had been threatened. The FBI was informed. The threat to Barnett had come in the form of a letter mailed from Boston, a protest of his failure to call Ed Armbrister for interference in the third game.

"I'm scared to death," Larry Barnett admitted.

Tuesday the Reds awoke and looked out the windows of their hotel. "Every morning it's the same thing," said Pete Rose. "I get up and look out to see if the windshield wipers are going on the cars." On this morning the wipers were still. The sun was shining. There was going to be a ballgame—the sixth game of the World Series, a game that was to go down as one of the greatest in World Series history.

Johnny Bench sat at the end of the bench before the game. "It's been a little hard waiting," he said. He thought about Gary Nolan, now on the spot, who he had grown up with in the Cincinnati organization.

"I've got to think about keeping the ball in the ball park," he said. But he couldn't do it. Gary Nolan gave up a three-run homer to Fred Lynn in the first inning. By the third inning Gary Nolan was gone and Luis Tiant was putting zeroes on the board.

But Tiant was not overpowering. The Reds were hitting him hard. They knew it was only a matter of time until they got to him and that time came in the fifth inning when Ken Griffey doubled in two runs, Lynn smashing into the wall and lying motionless for what seemed like an hour as an eerie silence fell over Fenway Park.

When Lynn recovered and remained in the game, Bench bailed Nolan out by hitting a single that tied the score, 3-3. It remained tied into the seventh inning. Then George Foster doubled off The Green Monster in centerfield and the Reds led 5-3. And in the eighth inning they increased it to 6-3 when Cesar Geronimo drove Tiant from the game with a home run.

Darrell Johnson had gone as long as was possible with Tiant, his Number 1 pitcher. Now he was gone and it was 6-3. The Big Red Machine was six outs from the world championship.

Pedro Borbon was pitching for the Reds. He gave up a single and a walk in the bottom of the eighth and exited in favor of Rawly Eastwick. Eastwick already had his foot in the door of the car awarded the series' most valuable player with two wins and a save. The door was to slam on his leg.

He struck out Dwight Evans and retired Rick Burleson on a fly to left. He was four outs away from winning it all. Bernie Carbo was sent up to pinch-hit and Anderson had a decision to make. Will McEnaney was loose in the Cincinnati bull pen, a left-handed pitcher. Anderson could have brought him in.

"If I had," Anderson explained, "they would have pinch-hit with Juan Beniquez. With that wall in left field, any right-handed hitter is a dangerous hitter. If Beniquez had come up and hit one over the wall I'd have been sick."

So he let Eastwick, his Number 1 pitcher, go against Carbo. Bernie Carbo, once like a son to Sparky Anderson but peddled away in 1971, drove one over the centerfield fence. The game was tied. The ninth inning came and went as did the tenth. And then it was the eleventh, one out, Ken Griffey on first base and Joe Morgan at the plate.

Joe Morgan, having a year that seemed to destine him to be the World Series hero, swung and sent a tremendous drive to right field that looked as if it were a home run. Dwight Evans turned his back to the plate and raced toward the wall. At the last second he threw his glove up and the baseball settled into it. It was one of the great catches of World Series history and Ken Griffey was doubled off first base.

Instead of being a hero, Morgan went to the field to play defense. The eleventh inning became the twelfth, the Reds wasting an opportunity against Rick Wise.

Now it was the bottom of the twelfth and Pat Darcy, the eighth Cincinnati pitcher in a parade that started with Gary Nolan, went to the mound to start his third inning.

Carlton Fisk stepped in. Darcy threw a ball. Then he threw a pitch right into Fisk's power and the Boston catcher connected. The ball hugged the foul line as it traveled toward The Green Monster. Fisk took two steps out of the batter's box, then stopped. Frantically he waved his arms, hoping through some magic to get the ball to remain fair. It hit into the foul screen. Fair ball. Leaping every other step, Carlton Fisk raced around the bases. It was over. The Red Sox had forced a seventh game.

After four days of rain and four hours and one minute, game Number 6 was history and it was worth waiting for.

Boston lived. The Cincinnati Reds sat quietly in their locker room, all except for Pete Rose. "The greatest game I've ever played in. Absolutely the greatest. Think what that will do for baseball. I'm just proud to be a part of the game."

Joe Morgan looked at the can of beer in his locker. "Beer today, champagne tomorrow," he said, sounding like the proprietor of a liquor store in Oakland, California.

And how right he was to be! The next day the team that could not win the big game won the biggest game of all. They won when Denny Doyle failed to turn a double play, allowing Tony Perez to hit a home run. And they won it on a bloop single by Joe Morgan, the man who was destined to be a World Series hero. His "almost" home run, caught by Evans, was now forgotten.

The Big Red Machine at long last could say they were the best in baseball.

"The sweetest taste in the world," said Johnny Bench as he sipped on some champagne.

It should have been the sweetest taste in the world. It had aged for thirty-five years.